The Simple Crock Pot Cookbook for Beginners

120 Easy, Delicious, and Healthy Recipes for Your Slow Cooker

Lindsey Page

© Text Copyright 2023 by Lindsey Page - All rights reserved.

This document is geared towards providing exact and reliable information in regards to the topic and issue covered. The publication is sold with the idea that the publisher is not required to render accounting, officially permitted, or otherwise, qualified services. If advice is necessary, legal or professional, a practiced individual in the profession should be ordered.

From a Declaration of Principles which was accepted and approved equally by a Committee of the American Bar Association and a Committee of Publishers and Associations.

In no way is it legal to reproduce, duplicate, or transmit any part of this document in either electronic means or in printed format. Recording of this publication is strictly prohibited and any storage of this document is not allowed unless with written permission from the publisher. All rights reserved.

The information provided herein is stated to be truthful and consistent, in that any liability, in terms of inattention or otherwise, by any usage or abuse of any policies, processes, or directions contained within is the solitary and utter responsibility of the recipient reader. Under no circumstances will any legal responsibility or blame be held against the publisher for any reparation, damages, or monetary loss due to the information herein, either directly or indirectly.

Respective authors own all copyrights not held by the publisher.

The information herein is offered for informational purposes solely, and is universal as so. The presentation of the information is without contract or any type of guarantee assurance.

The trademarks that are used are without any consent, and the publication of the trademark is without permission or backing by the trademark owner. All trademarks and brands within this book are for clarifying purposes only and are owned by the owners themselves, not affiliated with this document.

Table of Contents

CHAPTER ONE

Introduction of the Crock Pot 1

    Benefits of Using a Crock Pot 1
    How to Use a Crock Pot 2
    Tips for Crock Pot Cooking 3

CHAPTER TWO

Breakfast 5

    Spinach Frittata 5
    Breakfast Casserole 7
    Oats, Nuts, and Seeds Granola 9
    Meat and Veggie Casserole 11
    Apple French Toast Casserole 12
    Cauliflower Hash Brown Egg Cups 14
    Nutty Pumpkin Bread 15
    Veggie Omelet 17
    Easy Frittata 18
    Banana and Pecan Oatmeal 19
    Sweet Sausage and Peppers 21
    Vanilla Tapioca Pudding 22
    Spinach Quiche 23
    Apple Pie Quinoa Porridge 24
    Cheesy Grits 26
    Chocolate Oatmeal 27
    Broccoli Chop Breakfast 28

CHAPTER THREE

Vegetables and Beans 29

    Squash and Lentil Stew 29
    Vegetable Curry 30
    Stuffed Mushrooms 31
    Apples and Sweet Potatoes 32

Quinoa and Beans Chili 33
Potato, Pumpkin, and Beans Soup 34
Potato Salad 35
Broccoli Cauliflower "Rice" 36
Squash with Apples and Cranberries 37
Cheesy Cauliflower Puree 38
Eggplant and Tomato Sauce Paste 39
Garlic Mushrooms 40
Veggies with Quinoa and Beans 42
Sausage and Beans 43
Creamy Broccoli Soup 45
Zucchini Gratin 46
Coconut Creamed Spinach 47
Italian Zucchini and Yellow Squash 48

CHAPTER FOUR

Poultry 49

Pesto Chicken 49
Turkey Chili 51
Chicken Broccoli 52
Parmesan Chicken 53
Ranch Chicken 55
Chicken Stew 57
Honey-Glazed Chicken 58
Roasted Whole Chicken 59
Buffalo Chicken 60
Asian Chicken 61
Chicken Tortillas 62
Chicken and Beans Salad 63
Citrus Chicken 65
Salsa Chicken 66
Orange Sauce Meatballs 67
Turkey Burritos 69
Bacon-Wrapped Turkey Breast with Tomatoes 71
Slow-Cooked Turkey Breast 72
Turkey Meatloaf 73

CHAPTER FIVE

Meats **74**

    Spicy Beef Brisket 74
    Herbed Pork with Carrots 76
    Beef Curry 77
    Beef and Cabbage Stew 79
    Korean Beef Stew 80
    Miraculous Meatloaf 81
    Italian Meatballs 82
    Hungarian Goulash 83
    Mississippi Roast 85
    Braised Short Ribs 86
    Cabbage and Ribs 87
    Barbecue Beef Stew 88
    Slow Cooker Chili 90
    Paprika Pork 91
    Doughless Pizza 93
    Pork Burgers 94
    Country Style Pork Ribs 96
    Pulled Pork 97
    Pork Chops with Spice Rub 98
    Roasted Leg of Lamb 99
    Mustard Rosemary Lamb 100
    Balsamic Lamb Leg 101
    Braised Lamb 102
    Moroccan Lamb Stew 103
    Venison Steak and Veggies 104

CHAPTER SIX

Fish and Seafood **105**

    Lemon Tuna Steaks 105
    Seafood Stew 106
    Salmon with Wine Sauce 107
    Indonesian Fish 108
    Poached Salmon 109
    Citrus Salmon 111
    Spicy Mussels 113
    Shrimp Scampi 114

Polenta with Shrimp 115
Spicy Shrimp 117
Lemon Pepper Tilapia with Asparagus 118
Fish Curry 119
Lemon Herbed Tilapia 120
Chinese-Style Salmon 121
Spicy Seafood Stew 122
Lemon Pepper Cod with Asparagus 124

CHAPTER SEVEN

Soups 125

Cauliflower and Ham Soup 125
Vegetable Chickpea Soup 127
Kale Chicken Soup 128
Jalapeño Popper Soup 130
Cabbage Roll Soup 132
Vegetable Soup 134
Beef Cabbage Soup 135
Beef Bone Broth 136
Pizza Soup 137
Taco Soup 138
Bacon Soup 139
Chicken Noodle Soup 140

CHAPTER EIGHT

Snacks and Dessert 142

Mushroom Dip 142
Artichoke and Spinach Dip 144
Buffalo Chicken Wings 145
Buffalo Chicken Dip 146
Lemon Garlic Chicken Kebabs 147
Mushrooms in Wine Sauce 148
Apple Cake 149
Pumpkin Custard 151
Chocolate Pudding Cake 152
Peach Cobbler 154
Coconut Rice Pudding 156

Warm Fruit Compote 157
Fruit and Honey 158
Conclusion **159**
Check Out My Other Books **160**

CHAPTER ONE

Introduction of the Crock Pot

The Crock Pot has become a staple in kitchens worldwide for its convenience and simplicity. It is a slow cooker initially developed by the Naxon Corporation. When the company was purchased by The Rival Company, the product was introduced with the Crock Pot name in 1971. Since then, its popularity has grown steadily over the decades.

One of the most significant features of the Crock Pot is its ease of use. The original design was simple: an earthenware pot housed in a metal casing with a glass lid on top. It had a simple control knob for temperature settings and was low maintenance. You simply had to put in the ingredients, set the temperature, and let it cook. Over the years, Crock Pots have incorporated electronic controls, programmable settings, and even smartphone connectivity, but the core simplicity remains.

Benefits of Using a Crock Pot

For most people, the most important benefit of a Crock Pot is convenience. Using one pot to cook an entire meal is easier than cooking with several pots and pans. A full meal can be prepared in just a few minutes. People who have full-time jobs, attend school or have other time-consuming responsibilities can start the meal in the morning and know it will be ready to eat when they come home.

A Crock Pot is much safer than traditional stoves and ovens. Using a Crock Pot correctly will not risk being burned, and there is no fire risk.

Saving money is another benefit. You do not need to buy expensive cuts of your favorite meats because cheaper cuts will become tender, and the meat will never be tough or dry. You will also save money because washing a Crock Pot uses much less water than washing many pots and pans.

Personal taste is an additional benefit of slow cookers. When the flavors of all the foods in the pot blend, you will have a delicious meal.

How to Use a Crock Pot

It is always wise to read the instructions on a new appliance, but a slow cooker is quite simple.

First, consider safety. Make sure your outlet and wiring are in good condition so that the pot will not be a fire hazard. Always use the pot on a clean, dry surface, and never allow the cord to come in contact with water.

Do not allow children to play near the pot or open it to peek inside. The steam from a slow cooker is hot. Exercise care when you open the pot and remove the food. As the liquid is very hot, it is easy to burn yourself if you are not careful.

Use the amount of water recommended in the recipe. Never fill the pot with water.

Second, familiarize yourself with the settings. The Low setting is generally used for foods you wish to simmer. The High setting is for foods you would normally fry, boil, or bake. For the most flavorful dishes, try the Low setting. Food will cook completely in the gentle heat. The Warm setting is intended to keep food warm after it is cooked.

A third consideration is cleaning and maintaining your Crock Pot. As the pot rarely requires maintenance, all you need to do is clean it after use. While you can wash the pot and lid in the sink, never immerse the metal housing in water. If food or other residues need to be removed from the housing, use a moist cloth after unplugging the appliance.

Tips for Crock Pot Cooking

Layering is Key
Root vegetables such as potatoes, carrots, and onions usually take longer to cook. Place them at the bottom, closer to the heat source.
Lay your choice of meat on top of the vegetables to allow the juices to trickle down, enhancing flavor.

Liquids and Seasoning
The Crock Pot does not cause water to evaporate. If you are not using a recipe specially created for slow cookers, only add enough water to cover the food.
Don't be shy with herbs and spices. Flavors tend to dull over long cooking periods, so a little extra seasoning goes a long way.

Prepping Beforehand
Though not a mandatory step, browning meat before adding it to the Crock Pot can seal in flavor and give your dish a better texture.
Always thaw frozen ingredients before adding them to the Crock Pot. This ensures even cooking and minimizes the risk of bacterial growth.

Don't Overcrowd
Filling the Crock Pot too full can lead to uneven cooking. Aim to fill it no more than two-thirds full.

Stir Sparingly
Every time you lift the lid, you let out heat and extend the cooking time. Stir only when necessary.

Add Dairy Last
If your recipe includes dairy or coconut milk, add these last to prevent them from curdling.

Leftovers
Refrigerate leftovers promptly. Foods left to cool in the Crock Pot can encourage bacterial growth.

Feel free to experiment with your Crock Pot. In this book, you will find 120 healthy and delicious Crock Pot recipes that contain nutritional information. With a bit of practice, you will see that virtually every food you like can be cooked in this appliance.

CHAPTER TWO

Breakfast

Spinach Frittata

Servings: 6
Cooking Time: 2 hours
Ingredients:
8 large eggs
1 cup milk
1 (10-ounce) package frozen spinach, thawed and well-drained
1 cup shredded cheddar cheese
1 small onion, finely chopped
1 bell pepper, finely chopped
1 teaspoon salt
½ teaspoon black pepper
½ teaspoon garlic powder
½ teaspoon paprika

Directions:
1. Lightly grease the Crock Pot with nonstick cooking spray.
2. In a large bowl, whisk together the eggs and milk.
3. Add the spinach, onion, bell pepper, salt, black pepper, garlic powder, and paprika to the egg mixture. Mix well to combine.
4. Stir in the shredded cheese.
5. Carefully pour the mixture into the Crock Pot.
6. Set the Crock Pot on High. Cover and cook for about 1½–2 hours or until the desired doneness of eggs.
7. Turn off the Crock Pot and remove the lid. Let the frittata sit for about 5 minutes to make slicing easier. Serve warm.

Nutritional Information (Per Serving)
Calories: 209

Fat: 14.0g
Sat Fat: 6.6g
Carbohydrates: 6.6g
Fiber: 1.5g
Sugar: 4.1g
Protein: 15.6g
Sodium: 658mg

Breakfast Casserole

Servings: 8
Cooking Time: 7–8 hours
Ingredients:
12 large eggs
1 cup milk
Salt and pepper to taste
1 cup green bell pepper, chopped
2 ounces shallots, chopped
2 cups white mushrooms, chopped
16 large kale leaves, discard hard stem and ribs, finely chopped
6 slices bacon, chopped
1 tablespoon butter, melted
1 cup Parmesan cheese, shredded

Directions:
1. In a bowl, add the eggs, milk, salt, and pepper, and beat until well combined.
2. Add bacon to a skillet. Place the skillet over medium heat. Cook until the bacon is crisp.
3. Stir in the green pepper, shallots, and mushrooms. Sauté for 1–2 minutes.
4. Add kale and stir. Turn off the heat.
5. Grease the inside of the Crock Pot with butter. Transfer the vegetable mixture to the pot.
6. Sprinkle with cheese. Add the egg mixture and stir to combine.
7. Close the lid. Set the Crock Pot on Low and cook for 7–8 hours or until set.

Nutritional Information (Per Serving)
Calories: 278
Fat: 18g
Sat Fat: 7.2g
Carbohydrates: 9.1g
Fiber: 0.9g
Sugar: 3g

Protein: 21.2g

Oats, Nuts, and Seeds Granola

Servings: 14
Cooking Time: 2½ hours
Ingredients:
4 cups old-fashioned rolled oats
¼ cup almonds, chopped
¼ cup walnuts, chopped
¼ cup sunflower seeds
¼ cup pumpkin seeds
¼ cup brown sugar
½ teaspoon ground cinnamon
¼ teaspoon salt
½ cup coconut oil
½ cup honey
1 tablespoon vanilla extract
½ cup raisins

Directions:
1. Grease a Crock Pot with cooking spray. Add oats, nuts, seeds, brown sugar, cinnamon, and salt, and mix well.
2. In a bowl, add the remaining ingredients except for raisins and mix until well combined.
3. Pour the honey mixture over the oat mixture, and stir to combine well.
4. Set the Crock Pot on High. Cover the Crock Pot partially, and cook for about 2½ hours, stirring every 30 minutes.
5. Turn off the Crock Pot and immediately stir in raisins.
6. Transfer the granola to a large baking sheet, and set it aside at room temperature to cool completely.
7. Serve this granola with milk and your desired topping.
8. You can preserve this granola in an airtight container.

Nutritional Information (Per Serving)
Calories: 263
Fat: 13.1g
Sat Fat: 7.4g

Carbohydrates: 33.8g
Fiber: 3.1g
Sugar: 16g
Protein: 4.9g
Sodium: 46mg

Meat and Veggie Casserole

Servings: 12
Cooking Time: 6 hours
Ingredients:
3 cups sweet potatoes, sliced
1 pound breakfast sausage, crumbled
2 cups zucchini squash, sliced
6 green onions, sliced
12 eggs
¼ cup water
Salt and pepper to taste

Directions:
1. Heat the sausage in a skillet until brown.
2. Line the bottom of your Crock Pot with a disposable liner.
3. Place the sliced sweet potatoes on the bottom and cover them with the cooked sausage. Add the zucchini and onions.
4. Beat the eggs with the water and add salt and pepper. Pour into the Crock Pot.
5. Cook for 6 hours on the Low setting.

Nutritional Information (Per Serving)
Calories: 241
Fat: 15.2g
Sat Fat: 4.8g
Carbohydrates: 12.0g
Fiber: 2g
Sugar: 1.1g
Protein: 13.8g

Apple French Toast Casserole

Servings: 6
Cooking Time: 6–8 hours
Ingredients:
5 eggs
¾ cup half-and-half
¾ cup milk
¼ cup brown sugar, divided
1¾ teaspoons ground cinnamon
1 teaspoon vanilla extract
Pinch of salt
8 whole-grain bread slices, halved diagonally
3 medium apples, peeled, cored, and sliced thinly
¼ cup almonds, toasted and chopped

Directions:
1. Lightly grease the Crock Pot with nonstick cooking spray.
2. In a bowl, add eggs, half-and-half, milk, 3 tablespoons of brown sugar, cinnamon, vanilla extract, and salt, and beat until well combined.
3. Arrange the bread slices in the bottom of the prepared Crock Pot.
4. Place the apple slices over the bread slices. Pour the egg mixture evenly over the apple slices.
5. Sprinkle with the remaining brown sugar.
6. Set the Crock Pot on Low. Cover and cook for about 6–8 hours.
7. Uncover and set aside to cool for about 20 minutes before serving.
8. Cut into slices of equal size, and serve with a topping of almonds.

Nutritional Information (Per Serving)
Calories: 301
Fat: 11.2g
Sat Fat: 4.2g

Carbohydrates: 42.6g
Fiber: 6.2g
Sugar: 22.1g
Protein: 11.7g
Sodium: 308mg

Cauliflower Hash Brown Egg Cups

Servings: 6
Cooking Time: 6 hours
Ingredients:
1 head cauliflower, grated to a rice-like texture
¼ cup cheddar cheese or Mozzarella cheese
7 eggs
2 tablespoons Parmesan cheese, grated
Salt and pepper to taste
¼ teaspoon garlic powder

Directions:
1. Grease 6 muffin cups with cooking spray.
2. Lightly steam the cauliflower. Squeeze the cauliflower of excess moisture. Add into a bowl. Add 1 egg, cheese, salt, pepper, and garlic powder and mix well.
3. Divide into the 6 muffin cups. Press it into the cups making a well in each cup.
4. Place crumpled aluminum foil at the bottom of the Crock Pot (this step can be avoided if your pot is ceramic). Place the muffin molds inside the pot.
5. Close the lid. Set the pot on High and cook for 4 hours.
6. Open the lid and crack an egg in each muffin cup. Sprinkle with salt and pepper.
7. Cook on High for 2 hours or until the eggs are set.
8. Cool for a while. Run a knife around the edges of the egg cups. Remove them carefully and serve.

Nutritional Information (Per Serving)
Calories: 110
Fat: 7.1g
Sat Fat: 2.9g
Carbohydrates: 3g
Fiber: 1.1g
Sugar: 1.5g
Protein: 9.1g

Nutty Pumpkin Bread

Servings: 10
Cooking Time: 2 hours
Ingredients:
1 cup whole-wheat flour
1 cup all-purpose flour
1 teaspoon baking soda
½ teaspoon ground cinnamon
¼ teaspoon ginger, minced
Pinch of ground nutmeg
Salt to taste
2 eggs
2/3 cup maple syrup
½ cup canola oil
1 tablespoon milk
1 teaspoon vanilla extract
1 cup canned pumpkin puree
½ cup mini dark chocolate chips
½ cup walnuts, chopped

Directions:
1. Grease a loaf pan that fits inside a large Crock Pot.
2. In a large bowl, add flours, baking powder, spices, and salt, and mix well.
3. In another bowl, add eggs, maple syrup, oil, milk, and vanilla extract, and beat until well combined. Add pumpkin puree, and beat until well combined.
4. Add the egg mixture to the flour mixture, and mix until well combined.
5. Fold in chocolate chips and walnuts.
6. Transfer the mixture to the prepared loaf pan. Carefully arrange the loaf pan in the Crock Pot.
7. Set the Crock Pot on High. Cover it, and cook for about 2 hours or until a toothpick inserted in the center comes out clean.
8. Remove the loaf pan from the Crock Pot, and place it on a wire rack to cool for about 10 minutes.

9. Carefully invert the bread onto the wire rack, and cool completely before slicing.

Nutritional Information (Per Serving)
Calories: 374
Fat: 19.9g
Sat Fat: 3.5g
Carbohydrates: 46.9g
Fiber: 3.2g
Sugar: 24.5g
Protein: 6.1g

Veggie Omelet

Servings: 4
Cooking Time: 2 hours
Ingredients:
½ cup milk
6 eggs
⅛ teaspoon red chili powder
⅛ teaspoon garlic powder
Salt and pepper to taste
1 medium red bell pepper, seeded and sliced thinly
1 cup broccoli florets
1 small yellow onion, chopped
2 tablespoons fresh parsley, chopped

Directions:
1. In a bowl, add milk, eggs, chili powder, garlic powder, salt, and black pepper, and beat until well combined.
2. Lightly grease a Crock Pot. In the bottom of the Crock Pot, mix the bell pepper, broccoli, and onion.
3. Pour egg mixture on top and gently stir to combine.
4. Set the Crock Pot on High. Cover and cook for about 1½–2 hours or until the desired doneness of eggs.
5. Transfer the omelet onto a serving plate. Carefully cut into 4 wedges of equal size.
6. Serve hot with a garnish of parsley.

Nutritional Information (Per Serving)
Calories: 135
Fat: 7.4g
Sat Fat: 2.4g
Carbohydrates: 7.6g
Fiber: 1.5g
Sugar: 4.6g
Protein: 10.5g

Easy Frittata

Servings: 8
Cooking Time: 8–9 hours
Ingredients:
12 large eggs, beaten
1 cup milk
1½ cups artichoke hearts, chopped
½ cup green bell pepper, chopped
Salt and pepper to taste
1 tomato, deseeded, chopped
½ cup green onion, chopped
½ cup cheddar cheese, grated

Directions:
1. Spray the bottom of the Crock Pot with cooking spray.
2. Add all the ingredients except cheese into a bowl and mix well. Pour into the Crock Pot.
3. Close the lid. Set the pot on Low and cook for 8–9 hours or until the desired doneness of eggs.
4. Sprinkle cheese on top. Cover and let it sit for a few minutes.
5. Slice into 8 wedges and serve.

Nutritional Information (Per Serving)
Calories: 162
Fat: 10.5g
Sat Fat: 4.2g
Carbohydrates: 4.8g
Fiber: 0.7g
Sugar: 3.1g
Protein: 12.7g

Banana and Pecan Oatmeal

Servings: 8
Cooking Time: 7–8 hours
Ingredients:
2 cups old-fashioned oats
4 cups water
2 cups milk
3 ripe bananas, sliced
1 cup chopped pecans
¼ cup brown sugar
1 teaspoon vanilla extract
1 teaspoon ground cinnamon
¼ teaspoon salt

Directions:
1. Lightly grease the Crock Pot with nonstick cooking spray.
2. In a bowl, combine the oats, chopped pecans, brown sugar, ground cinnamon, and salt.
3. Transfer the dry mixture to the Crock Pot.
4. Add the sliced bananas, vanilla extract, water, and milk into the Crock Pot. Stir until well combined.
5. Set the Crock Pot on Low. Cover and cook for 7–8 hours, ideally overnight.
6. Serve hot with a topping of banana slices, pecans, or a dollop of yogurt.

Nutritional Information (Per Serving)
Calories: 262
Fat: 12.4g
Sat Fat: 1.9g
Carbohydrates: 34.5g
Fiber: 4.4g
Sugar: 15.8g
Protein: 6.2g
Sodium: 100mg

Sweet Sausage and Peppers

Servings: 6
Cooking Time: 2 hours 10 minutes
Ingredients:
12 ounces breakfast sausage, cut into pieces
1 cup red onion, sliced
2 cups mushrooms, sliced
2 cups bell pepper in any color, chopped
1 teaspoon olive oil
¼ cup water
2 teaspoons fresh parsley
2 teaspoons fresh tarragon

Directions:
1. Brown your sausage in a skillet for five minutes, and then stir the onion in the same skillet with the olive oil until it starts to soften.
2. Combine the sausage, onion, and mushrooms in the Crock Pot. Pour the water over the top.
3. Cover the Crock Pot, and let it cook on High for an hour.
4. Stir in the bell peppers, and allow them to cook for one more hour.
5. Sprinkle with parsley and tarragon before serving.

Nutritional Information (Per Serving)
Calories: 243
Fat: 18.6g
Sat Fat: 6.3g
Carbohydrates: 6.3g
Fiber: 1.2g
Sugar: 2.0g
Protein: 12.6g
Sodium: 736mg

Vanilla Tapioca Pudding

Servings: 8
Cooking Time: 6 hours
Ingredients:
2 eggs, beaten lightly
4 cups milk
2/3 cup sugar
½ cup small pearl tapioca
1 teaspoon vanilla extract
¼ teaspoon ground cinnamon
½ cup fresh blueberries

Directions:
1. In a Crock Pot, add all ingredients except blueberries, and mix until well combined.
2. Set the Crock Pot on Low.
3. Cover and cook for about 6 hours.
4. Serve warm with a topping of blueberries.

Nutritional Information (Per Serving)
Calories: 196
Fat: 5.1g
Sat Fat: 2.9g
Carbohydrates: 32.2g
Fiber: 0.3g
Sugar: 23.3g
Protein: 6.5g
Sodium: 76mg

Spinach Quiche

Servings: 4
Cooking Time: 4 hours
Ingredients:
10 ounces frozen chopped spinach, thawed and squeezed
4 ounces feta cheese, shredded
2 cups milk
4 eggs
¼ teaspoon red pepper flakes, crushed
Salt and pepper to taste

Directions:
1. In a Crock Pot, add all ingredients, and mix until well combined.
2. Set the Crock Pot on Low. Cover and cook for about 4 hours.

Nutritional Information (Per Serving)
Calories: 215
Fat: 13.2g
Sat Fat: 7.1g
Carbohydrates: 10.1g
Fiber: 1.6g
Sugar: 7.3g
Protein: 15.6g

Apple Pie Quinoa Porridge

Servings: 5
Cooking Time: 8 hours
Ingredients:

For Porridge:
1 cup uncooked quinoa, rinsed under cold water
1 apple, cored and chopped
3 tablespoons flax meal
3½ cups unsweetened soy milk
2 tablespoons pure maple syrup
1 tablespoon coconut oil, melted
1 teaspoon vanilla extract
1 teaspoon ground cinnamon
⅛ teaspoon ginger, minced
Pinch of ground cloves
Pinch of ground cardamom
Pinch of ground nutmeg
Salt to taste

For Topping:
1 apple, cored and sliced
3 tablespoons dried cranberries
3 tablespoons pecans, chopped

Directions:
1. Lightly grease the Crock Pot with nonstick cooking spray. Add quinoa, chopped apple, flax meal, soy milk, maple syrup, coconut oil, vanilla extract, spices, and salt, and stir to combine well.
2. Set the Crock Pot on Low. Cover and cook for about 8 hours.
3. Transfer the quinoa porridge to serving bowls.
4. Top with chopped apple, cranberries, and pecans.
5. If you like a creamier texture, pour in more milk while serving.

Nutritional Information (Per Serving)

Calories: 386
Fat: 14.3g
Sat Fat: 3.6g
Carbohydrates: 53.5g
Fiber: 7.9g
Sugar: 21.5g
Protein: 12.2g

Cheesy Grits

Servings: 8
Cooking Time: 8 hours
Ingredients:
1½ cups hand-ground grits
6 cups water
1 teaspoon salt
5 tablespoons butter
½ cup shredded Cheddar cheese; sharp Cheddar is great
Pepper to taste

Directions:
1. Lightly grease the inside of a Crock Pot, or coat with a nonstick spray.
2. Mix together the grits, water, and salt, and pour it into the Crock Pot.
3. Cook for 8 hours on Low.
4. Open the pot, and spoon in the butter in separate pieces.
5. Stir hard to combine the grits with the butter.
6. Add the shredded cheese and pepper.

Nutritional Information (Per Serving)
Calories: 201
Fat: 9.9g
Sat Fat: 6.1g
Carbohydrates: 23.4g
Fiber: 0.5g
Sugar: 0.2g
Protein: 4.4g
Sodium: 341mg

Chocolate Oatmeal

Servings: 4
Cooking Time: 3 hours
Ingredients:
4 cups water
½ cup unsweetened coconut milk
1 tablespoon cocoa powder
1 tablespoon maple syrup
1 teaspoon vanilla extract
¼ teaspoon salt
1 cup steel-cut oats
1 banana, peeled and sliced

Directions:
1. Lightly grease the Crock Pot with nonstick cooking spray.
2. In a large bowl, mix all ingredients except oats.
3. Spread oats in the bottom of the Crock Pot. Pour milk mixture evenly over oats.
4. Set the Crock Pot on High. Cover and cook for about 3 hours.
5. Serve hot with a topping of banana slices.

Nutritional Information (Per Serving)
Calories: 192
Fat: 8.8g
Sat Fat: 6.7g
Carbohydrates: 26.5g
Fiber: 3.9g
Sugar: 7.9g
Protein: 3.9g
Sodium: 307mg

Broccoli Chop Breakfast

Servings: 8
Cooking Time: 2–4 hours
Ingredients:
5 cups broccoli, chopped
12 ounces breakfast sausage, chopped
10 eggs
½ cup water
2 cloves garlic, sliced
Salt and pepper to taste

Directions:
1. Cook sausage in a skillet until brown.
2. Line your Crock Pot with a disposable liner and place half the broccoli on the bottom.
3. Put half the sausage on top of the broccoli and then add the rest of the broccoli and then the sausage, so it's layered.
4. Whisk together the eggs, garlic, water, salt, and pepper until combined, and pour over the ingredients in the pot.
5. Cook on High for 2 hours or Low for 4 hours.

Nutritional Information (Per Serving)
Calories: 243
Fat: 17.7g
Sat Fat: 5.6g
Carbohydrates: 4.5g
Fiber: 1.5g
Sugar: 1.4g
Protein: 16.8g

CHAPTER THREE

Vegetables and Beans

Squash and Lentil Stew

Servings: 6
Cooking Time: 6–8 hours
Ingredients:
1 large butternut squash, peeled and cubed
1 carrot, peeled and chopped
3 celery stalks, chopped
1 small onion, chopped
1 cup dried red lentils
½ teaspoon dried rosemary, crushed
Salt and pepper to taste
6 cups vegetable broth
¼ cup fresh parsley leaves, chopped

Directions:
1. In a Crock Pot, add all ingredients except parsley, and mix well.
2. Set the Crock Pot on Low. Cover and cook for 6–8 hours.
3. Top with parsley, and serve hot.

Nutritional Information (Per Serving)
Calories: 282
Fat: 2g
Sat Fat: 9.5g
Carbohydrates: 53.6g
Fiber: 15.8g
Sugar: 8.3g
Protein: 16.1g

Vegetable Curry

Servings: 4
Cooking Time: 4 hours 40 minutes
Ingredients:
1 green bell pepper, seeded and chopped
1 red bell pepper, seeded and chopped
2 sweet potatoes, peeled and cubed
1 cup carrot, peeled and chopped
1 (14 oz.) can coconut cream
2 tablespoons curry powder
2 tablespoons all-purpose flour
Salt and pepper to taste
1 cup fresh green peas, shelled
¼ cup fresh cilantro, chopped

Directions:
1. In a Crock Pot, add all ingredients except peas and cilantro, and mix well.
2. Set the Crock Pot on High. Cover and cook for about 3–4 hours.
3. Uncover the Crock Pot, add peas, and stir well.
4. Cover and cook for another 30–40 minutes.
5. Serve with a garnish of cilantro.

Nutritional Information (Per Serving)
Calories: 401
Fat: 24.6g
Sat Fat: 21.1g
Carbohydrates: 43.7g
Fiber: 9.8g
Sugar: 10.2g
Protein: 2g

Stuffed Mushrooms

Servings: 4
Cooking Time: 2–3 hours
Ingredients:
1 pound mushrooms
½ cup chicken broth
6 ounces Boursin cheese
Paprika to garnish

Directions:
1. Remove the stems from the mushrooms, and reserve them for another use.
2. Fill all the mushrooms with Boursin cheese, and place them at the bottom of the Crock Pot.
3. Pour some chicken broth around the mushrooms to fill the bottom of the pot. Sprinkle with paprika.
4. Close the lid. Set the pot on High and cook for 2–3 hours.
5. Serve hot.

Nutritional Information (Per Serving)
Calories: 199
Fat: 18.9g
Sat Fat: 12.8g
Carbohydrates: 5.2g
Fiber: 1.1g
Sugar: 3.4g
Protein: 7g
Sodium: 357mg

Apples and Sweet Potatoes

Servings: 8
Cooking Time: 6–7 hours
Ingredients:
4 large sweet potatoes, peeled and cut into 1-inch cubes
4 medium apples, cored and sliced
½ cup brown sugar
¼ cup maple syrup
½ cup apple juice
¼ cup unsalted butter, melted
1 teaspoon ground cinnamon
½ teaspoon ground nutmeg
¼ teaspoon salt

Directions:
1. Lightly grease the Crock Pot with nonstick cooking spray.
2. In the Crock Pot, layer half of the sweet potatoes, followed by half of the apple slices. Sprinkle half of the brown sugar, cinnamon, and nutmeg over the layer. Repeat with the remaining sweet potatoes and apples, followed by the remaining sugar and spices.
3. Pour the apple juice evenly over the layers. Drizzle the melted butter and maple syrup on top.
4. Set the Crock Pot on Low. Cover and cook for 6–7 hours.
5. Stir and serve warm.

Nutritional Information (Per Serving)
Calories: 240
Fat: 6g
Sat Fat: 3.7g
Carbohydrates: 47.9g
Fiber: 4g
Sugar: 33.4g
Protein: 1.3g
Sodium: 120mg

Quinoa and Beans Chili

Servings: 8
Cooking Time: 3½ hours
Ingredients:
1 (15 oz.) can red kidney beans, rinsed and drained
1 (15 oz.) can black beans, rinsed and drained
½ cup uncooked quinoa, rinsed
2 ounces canned chopped green chilies
1 (14 oz.) can diced tomatoes with juice
1 chipotle chili in adobo sauce, chopped
1 small onion, chopped
2 garlic cloves, minced
3 cups vegetable broth
1 tablespoon red chili powder
½ tablespoon ground cumin
½ teaspoon sugar
Salt and pepper to taste
2 tablespoons fresh lime juice
3 scallions, chopped

Directions:
1. In a large Crock Pot, add all ingredients except scallions, and mix well.
2. Set the Crock Pot on High. Cover and cook for about 3–3½ hours.
3. Garnish with scallion and serve.

Nutritional Information (Per Serving)
Calories: 461
Fat: 3.2g
Sat Fat: 0.6g
Carbohydrates: 83g
Fiber: 20.3g
Sugar: 7.9g
Protein: 8.5g

Potato, Pumpkin, and Beans Soup

Servings: 6
Cooking Time: 6–8 hours
Ingredients:
1 tablespoon vegetable oil
1 onion, chopped
1 potato, scrubbed and cubed
1 (15 oz.) can Great Northern Beans, rinsed and drained
¾ cup pumpkin puree
1 cup tomato puree
3 cups vegetable broth
¼ cup coconut milk
1 teaspoon dried rosemary, crushed
1 teaspoon ground cumin
½ teaspoon red pepper flakes, crushed
½ teaspoon paprika
Salt and pepper to taste
2 tablespoons fresh lime juice
¼ cup fresh cilantro leaves, chopped

Directions:
1. In a large Crock Pot, add all ingredients except cilantro leaves, and mix well.
2. Set the Crock Pot on Low. Cover and cook for about 6–8 hours.
3. Serve hot with a garnish of cilantro leaves.

Nutritional Information (Per Serving)
Calories: 384
Fat: 6.5g
Sat Fat: 3g
Carbohydrates: 63.9g
Fiber: 17.2g
Sugar: 7.2g
Protein: 20.4g

Potato Salad

Servings: 8
Cooking Time: 5–6 hours
Ingredients:
2 pounds red potatoes, peeled and sliced
1 teaspoon olive oil
1 cup celery, chopped
1 cup onion, chopped
½ cup green bell pepper, seeded and chopped
½ cup balsamic vinegar
¼ cup olive oil
3 tablespoons whole-grain mustard
6 cooked bacon slices, chopped
¼ cup fresh parsley, chopped

Directions:
1. In a Crock Pot, mix all ingredients except bacon and parsley.
2. Set the Crock Pot on Low. Cover and cook for about 5–6 hours.
3. Top with bacon and parsley, and serve immediately.

Nutritional Information (Per Serving)
Calories: 267
Fat: 16.1g
Sat Fat: 3.9g
Carbohydrates: 20.7g
Fiber: 2.5g
Sugar: 2g
Protein: 10.2g
Sodium: 530mg

Broccoli Cauliflower "Rice"

Servings: 8
Cooking Time: 2–3 hours
Ingredients:
1 pound cauliflower, grated
8 ounces broccoli, chopped
4–5 tablespoons water
4 tablespoons butter
1 tablespoon lemon zest, grated
2 cloves garlic, minced
½ teaspoon garlic salt or salt
¼ cup Parmesan cheese, grated
Pepper to taste
1 medium onion, minced

Directions:
1. Add cauliflower and broccoli into the Crock Pot. Sprinkle water over it.
2. Close the lid. Set the pot on High and cook for about 2–3 hours.
3. Add the rest of the ingredients and stir. Cover and set aside for a while for the flavors to set in.
4. Serve warm.

Nutritional Information (Per Serving)
Calories: 91
Fat: 6.5g
Sat Fat: 4.1g
Carbohydrates: 6.8g
Fiber: 2.5g
Sugar: 2.5g
Protein: 3.1g
Sodium: 94mg

Squash with Apples and Cranberries

Servings: 6
Cooking Time: 4 hours
Ingredients:
1 (3 lb.) butternut squash, peeled, seeded, and cut into cubes
3 apples, peeled, cored, and chopped
½ cup dried cranberries
½ white onion, chopped
1 tablespoon ground cinnamon
1 teaspoon ground nutmeg
Salt and pepper to taste

Directions:
1. In a large Crock Pot, add all ingredients and mix well.
2. Set the Crock Pot on High.
3. Cover and cook for about 4 hours.

Nutritional Information (Per Serving)
Calories: 173
Fat: 0.6g
Sat Fat: 0g
Carbohydrates: 44.7g
Fiber: 8.5g
Sugar: 17.4g
Protein: 2.7g

Cheesy Cauliflower Puree

Servings: 8
Cooking Time: 3 hours
Ingredients:
4 cups cauliflower florets
½ cup chicken broth
2 tablespoons butter
Salt and pepper to taste
4 ounces sharp cheese
¼ cup heavy cream

Directions:
1. Add all of the ingredients into the Crock Pot.
2. Close the lid. Set the pot on High and cook for 3 hours.
3. Blend with an immersion blender until smooth.
4. Serve warm.

Nutritional Information (Per Serving)
Calories: 108
Fat: 8.9g
Sat Fat: 5.7g
Carbohydrates: 3.3g
Fiber: 1.3g
Sugar: 1.2g
Protein: 4.9g

Eggplant and Tomato Sauce Paste

Servings: 6
Cooking Time: 5–7 hours
Ingredients:
1 medium eggplant, cut into ½" cubes
1 onion, chopped finely
4 garlic cloves, minced
2 (14 oz.) cans diced tomatoes, drained
1 (6 oz.) can tomato paste
½ cup red wine
2 teaspoons dried oregano, crushed
Salt and pepper to taste
1 pound uncooked penne pasta
¼ cup fresh parsley, chopped

Directions:
1. In a Crock Pot, add all ingredients except pasta and parsley.
2. Set the Crock Pot on Low. Cover and cook for about 5–7 hours.
3. In a pan of lightly salted boiling water, cook the pasta for about 8–10 minutes or according to the package's directions. Drain well and set aside.
4. Uncover the Crock Pot, add pasta, and gently stir to combine.
5. Serve immediately with a topping of parsley.

Nutritional Information (Per Serving)
Calories: 313
Fat: 2.4g
Sat Fat: 0g
Carbohydrates: 59.8g
Fiber: 6.2g
Sugar: 10.2g
Protein: 12.2g

Garlic Mushrooms

Servings: 3
Cooking Time: 2–3 hours
Ingredients:
1 pound white button mushrooms, quartered
3 garlic cloves, minced
¼ cup fresh parsley, chopped
Salt and pepper to taste
2 tablespoons butter, melted
1 teaspoon fresh lemon zest, grated finely

Directions:
1. In a Crock Pot, add all ingredients except lemon zest and butter, and mix well.
2. Set the slow cooker on High.
3. Cover and cook for 2–3 hours.
4. Uncover the Crock Pot, and drizzle with the melted butter.
5. Serve with a topping of lemon zest.

Nutritional Information (Per Serving)
Calories: 107
Fat: 8.2g
Sat Fat: 4.9g
Carbohydrates: 6.4g
Fiber: 1.8g
Sugar: 2.7g
Protein: 5.2g

Veggies with Quinoa and Beans

Servings: 5
Cooking Time: 4–6 hours
Ingredients:
1¼ cups uncooked quinoa, rinsed under cold water
1¼ cups canned black beans, rinsed and drained
1 cup fresh green beans, trimmed and chopped
1 small carrot, peeled and chopped
1 small orange bell pepper, seeded and chopped
1 small yellow bell pepper, seeded and chopped
1 small onion, chopped
2 garlic cloves, minced
3½ cups vegetable broth
Salt and pepper to taste
2 tablespoons fresh cilantro leaves, chopped

Directions:
1. In a Crock Pot, mix all ingredients except cilantro, and stir to combine.
2. Set the Crock Pot on Low. Cover and cook for 4–6 hours.
3. Uncover the Crock Pot, and with a fork, fluff the quinoa mixture.
4. Serve with a topping of cilantro.

Nutritional Information (Per Serving)
Calories: 382
Fat: 4.4g
Sat Fat: 0.8g
Carbohydrates: 66g
Fiber: 12.3g
Sugar: 5.3g
Protein: 21.1g

Sausage and Beans

Servings: 8
Cooking Time: 3–4 hours
Ingredients:
1 pound sausage, sliced into ½-inch pieces
3 cans (15 oz each) white beans, drained and rinsed
1 can (14½ oz) diced tomatoes, undrained
1 medium onion, finely chopped
3 cloves garlic, minced
1 green bell pepper, diced
1 cup chicken broth
2 teaspoon paprika
1 teaspoon ground cumin
1 teaspoon salt
½ teaspoon black pepper
1 tablespoon olive oil
¼ cup fresh parsley leaves, chopped

Directions:
1. In a skillet over medium heat, add 1 tablespoon of olive oil. Add the sausage and cook until lightly browned on both sides. Remove the sausage and set aside.
2. In the same skillet, add the onion, garlic, and green bell pepper. Sauté until the onion becomes translucent.
3. Transfer the mixture to the crock pot. Add the remaining ingredients. Stir well to combine.
4. Set the Crock Pot on High. Cover and cook for 3–4 hours.
5. Top with parsley, and serve hot.

Nutritional Information (Per Serving)
Calories: 349
Fat: 20.2g
Sat Fat: 6.8g
Carbohydrates: 26.4g
Fiber: 7.2g
Sugar: 3.8g
Protein: 16g

Sodium: 1189mg

Creamy Broccoli Soup

Servings: 6
Cooking Time: 3–4 hours
Ingredients:
1 medium onion, sliced
1 carrot, peeled and chopped
3 cups broccoli, chopped
2 garlic cloves, minced
¼ teaspoon cayenne pepper
1 teaspoon lemon juice
2 teaspoons all-purpose flour
½ teaspoon dried oregano, crushed
Salt and pepper to taste
4 cups chicken broth
1 cup heavy cream

Directions:
1. In a Crock Pot, add all ingredients except cream, and mix until well combined.
2. Set the Crock Pot on Low. Cover and cook for 3–4 hours.
3. Uncover and immediately add cream, and stir until well combined.
4. Serve hot.

Nutritional Information (Per Serving)
Calories: 127
Fat: 8.5g
Sat Fat: 4.9g
Carbohydrates: 8g
Fiber: 1.9g
Sugar: 2.6g
Protein: 5.4g
Sodium: 540mg

Zucchini Gratin

Servings: 4
Cooking Time: 2–3 hours
Ingredients:
2 cups zucchini slices
Salt and pepper to taste
1 tablespoon butter, melted
¼ cup heavy whipping cream
½ small onion, thinly sliced
¾ cup pepper Jack cheese, shredded
¼ teaspoon garlic powder

Directions:
1. Grease the inside of the Crock Pot with a bit of oil.
2. Place onion slices at the bottom of the pot. Layer with zucchini slices followed by cheese.
3. Mix the rest of the ingredients in a bowl and pour over the cheese layer.
4. Close the lid. Set the pot on High and cook for 2–3 hours or until zucchini is tender.
5. Let it sit for a while before serving. Slice into 4 equal portions and serve.

Nutritional Information (Per Serving)
Calories: 131
Fat: 11.2g
Sat Fat: 7.2g
Carbohydrates: 3.2g
Fiber: 0.9g
Sugar: 1.5g
Protein: 5.3g

Coconut Creamed Spinach

Servings: 4
Cooking Time: 2–3 hours
Ingredients:
½ cup coconut milk
¼ teaspoon ground nutmeg
¼ teaspoon cayenne pepper
8 cups baby spinach
Salt to taste

Directions:
1. Add all the ingredients to the Crock Pot.
2. Close the lid. Set the pot on Low and cook for 2–3 hours.
3. Stir and serve.

Nutritional Information (Per Serving)
Calories: 84
Fat: 7.5g
Sat Fat: 6.4g
Carbohydrates: 4g
Fiber: 2g
Sugar: 1.3g
Protein: 2.4g

Italian Zucchini and Yellow Squash

Servings: 3
Cooking Time: 5–6 hours
Ingredients:
1 medium yellow squash, quartered, sliced
1 medium zucchini, quartered, sliced
1 teaspoon Italian seasoning or to taste
¼ teaspoon sea salt
2 tablespoons Parmesan cheese, grated
Pepper to taste
½ teaspoon garlic powder
2 tablespoons cold butter, cubed

Directions:
1. Add squash and zucchini into the Crock Pot.
2. Sprinkle with salt, garlic powder, pepper, and Italian seasoning.
3. Place butter cubes all over the vegetables. Sprinkle cheese on top.
4. Close the lid. Set the pot on Low and cook for 5–6 hours or until tender.
5. Stir and serve.

Nutritional Information (Per Serving)
Calories: 107
Fat: 9.2g
Sat Fat: 5.5g
Carbohydrates: 5g
Fiber: 1.5g
Sugar: 2.5g
Protein: 3g
Sodium: 259mg

CHAPTER FOUR

Poultry

Pesto Chicken

Servings: 3
Cooking Time: 4 hours
Ingredients:
2 cups spinach, chopped
1 cup fresh basil leaves, chopped
½ cup walnuts
2 tablespoons olive oil
½ lemon, juiced
1 tablespoon parmesan cheese
¼ cup pine nuts
1 pound cooked chicken, shredded or cubed
2 garlic cloves
½ white onion, sliced
½ cup sundried tomatoes
1 cup chicken broth
Salt and pepper to taste

Directions:
1. In a bowl, mix the spinach, basil, walnuts, olive oil, and lemon juice until paste-like texture.
2. Place the chicken in your Crock Pot and cover with the pesto mix you just prepared.
3. Add the cheese, pine nuts, garlic, onion, and tomatoes.
4. Season with salt and pepper and then cover with the chicken broth.
5. Cook on Low for 4 hours.

Nutritional Information (Per Serving)

Calories: 574
Fat: 35.3g
Sat Fat: 4.3g
Carbohydrates: 12.9g
Fiber: 4g
Sugar: 6.1g
Protein: 55.1g

Turkey Chili

Servings: 6
Cooking Time: 7 hours
Ingredients:
2 tablespoons olive oil
4 cloves garlic, minced
1 green bell pepper, chopped
1 pound ground turkey
7½ ounces canned diced tomatoes
7½ ounces canned pumpkin puree
1 tablespoon chili powder
½ teaspoon ground cumin
½ teaspoon onion powder
3 ounces tomato paste
¾ cup chicken broth
1 teaspoon ground cinnamon
½ teaspoon sea salt or to taste
Freshly ground pepper to taste

Directions:
1. Place a skillet with oil over medium-high heat. Add pepper and garlic. Sauté for a couple of minutes until garlic turns aromatic.
2. Add ground turkey. Sauté until the meat is not pink anymore.
3. Transfer into the Crock Pot.
4. Add the rest of the ingredients and mix well.
5. Close the lid. Set the pot on Low and cook for 7 hours.
6. Ladle into bowls and serve.

Nutritional Information (Per Serving)
Calories: 307
Fat: 14.3g
Sat Fat: 2.4g
Carbohydrates: 26.3g
Fiber: 8.4g
Sugar: 13g
Protein: 25.8g
Sodium: 377mg

Chicken Broccoli

Servings: 4
Cooking Time: 4–5 hours
Ingredients:
1 pound skinless, boneless chicken thighs, cubed
1½ cups coconut milk
1 small white onion, chopped
2 garlic cloves, minced
2 cups broccoli, chopped
Salt and pepper to taste
1 tablespoon fresh lemon juice

Directions:
1. In a Crock Pot, add all ingredients except lemon juice, and mix well.
2. Set the Crock Pot on Low. Cover and cook for 4–5 hours.
3. Serve hot with a drizzling of lemon juice.

Nutritional Information (Per Serving)
Calories: 187
Fat: 6.5g
Sat Fat: 3.0g
Carbohydrates: 7.3g
Fiber: 1.7g
Sugar: 2.4g
Protein: 24.3g

Parmesan Chicken

Servings: 4
Cooking Time: 6 hours
Ingredients:
4 skinless, boneless chicken breasts
1 cup Parmesan cheese, grated
1 tablespoon Italian seasoning
1 teaspoon garlic powder
1 teaspoon onion powder
1 teaspoon salt
½ teaspoon black pepper
2 cups marinara sauce
1 cup mozzarella cheese, shredded

Directions:
1. In a small bowl, mix together the Parmesan cheese, Italian seasoning, garlic powder, onion powder, salt, and pepper.
2. Coat the chicken breasts evenly with the cheese mixture.
3. Place the chicken breasts in the Crock Pot.
4. Pour the marinara sauce over the top of the chicken.
5. Close the lid. Set the pot on Low and cook for 6 hours.
6. 30 minutes before serving, sprinkle the mozzarella cheese over the top of the chicken.
7. Close the lid and let the cheese melt.
8. Serve warm.

Nutritional Information (Per Serving)
Calories: 403
Fat: 19g
Sat Fat: 9.4g
Carbohydrates: 6g
Fiber: 1g
Sugar: 3.3g
Protein: 51.1g
Sodium: 1400mg

Ranch Chicken

Servings: 3
Cooking Time: 4 hours 45 minutes
Ingredients:
For ranch seasoning mix:
½ tablespoon dried parsley
¾ teaspoon dried dill
¼ teaspoon dried onion
¼ teaspoon salt
1 teaspoon dried chives
¼ teaspoon paprika
¼ teaspoon garlic powder
Freshly ground pepper to taste

For ranch chicken:
3 chicken breast halves, skinless and boneless
¾ teaspoon steak seasoning
2 teaspoons ranch seasoning mix (given above)
½ cup chicken broth
2 small shallots, sliced
6 slices bacon
3 cups broccoli florets
¼ cup mayonnaise
Salt to taste
1½ tablespoons red wine vinegar

Directions:
1. Mix all the ingredients of ranch seasoning in a small jar. Use 2 teaspoons of it.
2. Place chicken in the Crock Pot. Season the chicken with ranch seasoning and steak seasoning. Add the broth and place shallots on top.
3. Close the lid. Set the pot on Low and cook for 4 hours.
4. Add broccoli and cook for 45 minutes.
5. Meanwhile, cook the bacon in a skillet until crisp. Crumble the bacon when cooled.

6. When the chicken is done, shred it and add it back into the pot. Add vinegar, salt, bacon, and mayonnaise and mix well.

7. Serve warm.

Nutritional Information (Per Serving)
Calories: 442
Fat: 25.5g
Sat Fat: 6.2g
Carbohydrates: 13.1g
Fiber: 2.5g
Sugar: 3.1g
Protein: 39.1g

Chicken Stew

Servings: 2
Cooking Time: 6–8 hours
Ingredients:
1 cup chicken stock
2 cups chicken, skinless, boneless, chopped into chunks
1 stalk celery, chopped
3 cloves garlic, minced
¼ cup onion, chopped
¼ teaspoon dried rosemary
¼ teaspoon dried oregano
¼ teaspoon dried thyme
1 tablespoon olive oil
½ cup fresh spinach, chopped
Salt and pepper to taste
½ cup heavy cream
⅛ teaspoon xanthan gum

Directions:
1. Add celery, chicken, stock, garlic, onion, herbs, and olive oil into the Crock Pot and stir.
2. Close the lid, set the pot on Low, and cook for 6–8 hours.
3. Add spinach, salt, pepper, and cream.
4. Sprinkle some xanthan gum to get the desired thickness. Whisk well.
5. Heat thoroughly. Ladle into bowls and serve.

Nutritional Information (Per Serving)
Calories: 397
Fat: 22.7g
Sat Fat: 9.2g
Carbohydrates: 4.9g
Fiber: 1.4g
Sugar: 1.2g
Protein: 42.3g
Sodium: 530mg

Honey-Glazed Chicken

Servings: 6
Cooking Time: 6–8 hours
Ingredients:
2¼ pounds chicken pieces
1 medium onion, chopped
⅓ cup chives, minced
1½ tablespoons ginger, minced
3 tablespoons sherry
2½ tablespoons honey
1½ tablespoons soy sauce
2 tablespoons black sesame seeds, toasted

Directions:
1. In the bottom of a Crock Pot, place chicken pieces.
2. In a bowl, add the remaining ingredients except for sesame seeds, and mix well. Pour the mixture evenly over the chicken.
4. Set the Crock Pot on Low. Cover and cook for 6–8 hours.
6. Serve hot with a garnish of sesame seeds.

Nutritional Information (Per Serving)
Calories: 391
Fat: 14.2g
Sat Fat: 3.7g
Carbohydrates: 11.1g
Fiber: 1g
Sugar: 8.2g
Protein: 50.4g
Sodium: 374mg

Roasted Whole Chicken

Servings: 6
Cooking Time: 6–8 hours
Ingredients:
1 (3½ lb.) whole chicken, cleaned, pat dried
5 garlic cloves, peeled
1 large carrot, peeled and chopped
1 large celery stalk, chopped
1 medium onion, chopped
1 tablespoon Herbs de Provence
Salt and pepper to taste
3 tablespoons fresh lemon juice

Directions:
1. Stuff the chicken cavity with garlic cloves.
2. Sprinkle the chicken all over with salt, pepper, and Herbs de Provence.
3. In the bottom of a Crock Pot, place the vegetables.
4. Arrange the chicken over the vegetables. Drizzle with lemon juice.
5. Set the Crock Pot on Low. Cover and cook for 6–8 hours.
6. Serve with fresh baby greens.

Nutritional Information (Per Serving)
Calories: 520
Fat: 19.7g
Sat Fat: 5.5g
Carbohydrates: 3.7g
Fiber: 0.8g
Sugar: 1.5g
Protein: 77.1g

Buffalo Chicken

Servings: 3
Cooking Time: 7 hours
Ingredients:
3 chicken breasts
2 teaspoons ranch seasoning mix
½ cup hot sauce
1 tablespoon butter

Directions:
1. Place chicken in the Crock Pot. Drizzle hot sauce over it. Season with ranch seasoning.
2. Close the lid. Set the pot on Low and cook for 6 hours.
3. Remove the chicken with a slotted spoon. Shred the chicken and add it back into the pot.
4. Add butter and cook without the lid on Low for an hour.

Nutritional Information (Per Serving)
Calories: 155
Fat: 6.5g
Sat Fat: 2.5g
Carbohydrates: 0.7g
Fiber: 0.1g
Sugar: 0.5g
Protein: 21.4g
Sodium: 1168mg

Asian Chicken

Servings: 6
Cooking Time: 6 hours
Ingredients:
12 ounces chicken pieces (thighs work best)
1 cup shredded carrots
½ cup green onions, chopped
1 pound cabbage, shredded
5 cloves garlic, minced
1 tablespoon soy sauce
4 teaspoons sesame oil
2 tablespoons water
1 teaspoon white vinegar
1 teaspoon honey
1 tablespoon grated ginger

Directions:
1. Combine the ginger, honey, vinegar, water, sesame oil, garlic, and soy sauce in a small bowl.
2. Put the cabbage, onions, and carrots into the Crock Pot and combine.
3. Place the chicken on top of the cabbage and drizzle with the mixture from the bowl.
4. Cook on Low for 6 hours.

Nutritional Information (Per Serving)
Calories: 176
Fat: 7.4g
Sat Fat: 1.6g
Carbohydrates: 9.4g
Fiber: 2.7g
Sugar: 4.6g
Protein: 18.1g
Sodium: 228mg

Chicken Tortillas

Servings: 4
Cooking Time: 6–8 hours
Ingredients:
For Chicken:
1 cup chicken broth
1 (1¼ oz.) package dry taco seasoning mix
1 pound skinless, boneless chicken breasts

For Tortillas:
8 corn tortillas, warmed
1 cup purple cabbage, shredded
1 cup carrot, peeled and shredded
½ cup sour cream

Directions:
1. In a bowl, mix broth and taco seasoning.
2. In the Crock Pot, place chicken breasts and top with broth mixture.
3. Set the Crock Pot on Low. Cover and cook for 6–8 hours.
4. Uncover the Crock Pot, and with 2 forks, shred the chicken breasts. Mix completely with pan juices.
5. Divide the shredded chicken between warm tortillas. Top with cabbage, carrot, and sour cream and serve.

Nutritional Information (Per Serving)
Calories: 361
Fat: 11.8g
Sat Fat: 5.6g
Carbohydrates: 32.3g
Fiber: 4.1g
Sugar: 2.5g
Protein: 30.6g
Sodium: 799mg

Chicken and Beans Salad

Servings: 8
Cooking Time: 4–5 hours
Ingredients:
For Chicken:
2 (8 oz.) skinless, boneless chicken breasts
2 tablespoons taco seasoning
2 cups canned black beans, rinsed and drained
2 cups chunky salsa

For Dressing:
1 cup buttermilk
1 large avocado, peeled, pitted, and chopped roughly
1 jalapeño, seeded and chopped
3 tablespoons scallions, chopped
3 tablespoons fresh cilantro, chopped
1 tablespoon lime juice
⅛ teaspoon ground cumin
Salt and pepper to taste

For Salad:
8 cups romaine lettuce, chopped
⅓ cup cheddar cheese, shredded
½ cup scallions, chopped

Directions:
1. Season chicken evenly with taco seasoning.
2. In a Crock Pot, place chicken, followed by beans and salsa.
3. Set the Crock Pot on Low. Cover and cook for 4–5 hours.
4. Uncover the Crock Pot, and transfer the chicken into a bowl. Set aside to cool slightly.
5. Chop the chicken into bite-sized pieces. Return the chicken to the Crock Pot, and mix with beans and salsa.
6. For the dressing, in a blender, add all ingredients and pulse until smooth.

7. Divide lettuce onto serving plates. Top with the chicken mixture, followed by the cheese and dressing.

8. Serve immediately with a garnish of scallions.

Nutritional Information (Per Serving)
Calories: 470
Fat: 13.4g
Sat Fat: 4.5g
Carbohydrates: 54.4g
Fiber: 14.3g
Sugar: 6.8g
Protein: 36.8g
Sodium: 653mg

Citrus Chicken

Servings: 6
Cooking Time: 4 hours
Ingredients:
3 pounds chicken
2 limes, juiced
1 lemon, juiced
1 orange, juiced
4 tablespoons fresh cilantro
3 tomatoes, chopped
1 red onion, chopped
1 teaspoon red pepper flakes
Salt and pepper to taste

Directions:

1. Place the chicken at the bottom of the Crock Pot and add the citrus juice, tomatoes, onion, red pepper, and cilantro.

2. Stir everything together and cook on High for 4 hours. The chicken will be tender and easily shredded, and you'll love the tangy flavor.

Nutritional Information (Per Serving)
Calories: 287
Fat: 5.9g
Sat Fat: 0g
Carbohydrates: 7.7g
Fiber: 1.4g
Sugar: 4.8g
Protein: 48.5g

Salsa Chicken

Servings: 4
Cooking Time: 6 hours
Ingredients:
4 skinless chicken breasts
16 ounces mild salsa
1½ teaspoons dried parsley
½ teaspoon dried cilantro
1 teaspoon onion powder
½ teaspoon paprika
1 teaspoon garlic powder
¼ teaspoon black pepper
2 tablespoons water

Directions:
1. Put the chicken pieces at the bottom of your Crock Pot.
2. Add the spices, salsa, and water, and mix well.
3. Cook on Low for 6 hours.

Nutritional Information (Per Serving)
Calories: 276
Fat: 3.4g
Sat Fat: 0g
Carbohydrates: 6.7g
Fiber: 0.6g
Sugar: 3.8g
Protein: 53.6g
Sodium: 827mg

Orange Sauce Meatballs

Servings: 6
Cooking Time: 4–5 hours
Ingredients:
For Meatballs:
1 pound ground turkey
1 egg
2 teaspoons paprika
1 teaspoon ginger, minced
1 teaspoon ground cumin
1 teaspoon cayenne pepper
Salt and pepper to taste

For Sauce:
1 cup orange marmalade
¼ cup fresh orange juice
¼ cup chicken broth
1 small jalapeño, seeded and chopped finely
4 scallions, chopped
Salt and pepper to taste

For Topping:
2 tablespoons black sesame seeds
¼ cup scallions, chopped

Directions:
1. For meatballs, in a large bowl, add all ingredients and mix until well combined.
2. Make small balls of equal size from the turkey mixture.
3. In a Crock Pot, add all sauce ingredients, and mix well. Carefully place the meatballs in the sauce.
4. Set the Crock Pot on Low. Cover and cook for 4–5 hours.
5. Serve hot with a topping of sesame seeds and scallions.

Nutritional Information (Per Serving)
Calories: 352

Fat: 12.5g
Sat Fat: 3.1g
Carbohydrates: 39.3g
Fiber: 1.6g
Sugar: 33.5g
Protein: 23.0g

Turkey Burritos

Servings: 8
Cooking Time: 8 hours 30 minutes
Ingredients:
1 lb. ground turkey meat
2 tablespoons taco seasoning
1 cup corn kernels, fresh or frozen
1 can drained kidney beans
1 can crushed tomatoes
¾ cup chicken broth
2 cups brown rice
1 cup diced tomatoes
½ cup diced avocados
2 tablespoons chopped cilantro
2 teaspoons lime juice
Salt and pepper to taste
8 flour tortillas
3 cups shredded Cheddar cheese
1 cup sour cream

Directions:
1. Break up the turkey meat, and place it in the Crock Pot.
2. Season the meat with taco seasoning.
3. Add in the beans first, then the corn kernels, and, lastly, the crushed tomatoes.
4. Pour in the chicken broth.
5. Cook for 8 hours on Low.
6. Stir the ingredients well.
7. Stir in the rice, and stir some more.
8. Cook for another 15 minutes on High.
9. In a bowl, mix the avocado, lime juice, cilantro, salt, and pepper. Set aside.
10. Lay out the corn tortillas on the counter, and fill each with ½ cup turkey filling.
11. Roll up the tortillas, and put them on a baking sheet.
12. Distribute the cheese equally on top of each tortilla.

13. Set the broiler on High, and broil the tortillas for about 5 minutes. Don't let the cheese burn.

14. When serving, add the avocado salsa and sour cream.

Nutritional Information (Per Serving)
Calories: 618
Fat: 27.8g
Sat Fat: 13.5g
Carbohydrates: 61.7g
Fiber: 5.5g
Sugar: 2.8g
Protein: 30.5g
Sodium: 902mg

Bacon-Wrapped Turkey Breast with Tomatoes

Servings: 8
Cooking Time: 4 hours
Ingredients:
2 pounds turkey breast, chopped
6 tomatoes, peeled and chopped
2 bay leaves
16 ounces bacon slices, thinly cut
¼ teaspoon garlic powder
Salt and pepper to taste

Directions:
1. Take the bacon slices and wrap them around the turkey.
2. Add the rest of the ingredients into the Crock Pot and stir.
3. Place the turkey in the pot.
4. Close the lid. Set the pot on High and cook for 4 hours.
5. Discard bay leaves. Slice the turkey and serve with the cooked sauce.

Nutritional Information (Per Serving)
Calories: 295
Fat: 16.1g
Sat Fat: 5.4g
Carbohydrates: 8.5g
Fiber: 1.7g
Sugar: 6.4g
Protein: 30.2g

Slow-Cooked Turkey Breast

Servings: 6
Cooking Time: 8 hours
Ingredients:
2½ pounds bone-in skin-on turkey breast
2 tablespoons olive oil
3 tablespoons Stubbs' chicken spice rub mixture
½ cup chicken broth
Salt and pepper to taste

Directions:
1. Sprinkle salt and pepper over the turkey.
2. Place the turkey in the Crock Pot. Rub the olive oil and spice rub over it.
3. Add the broth and close the lid.
4. Set the pot on High and cook for 1 hour and then on Low for 7 hours.

Nutritional Information (Per Serving)
Calories: 365
Fat: 14.2g
Sat Fat: 3.8g
Carbohydrates: 0.1g
Fiber: 0g
Sugar: 0.1g
Protein: 55.8g

Turkey Meatloaf

Servings: 6
Cooking Time: 6 hours
Ingredients:
2 pounds ground turkey
1 cup breadcrumbs
½ cup milk
1 small onion, finely chopped
½ cup carrot, finely chopped
2 garlic cloves, minced
2 large eggs, beaten
¼ cup ketchup
2 tablespoons Worcestershire sauce
1 teaspoon dried thyme
1 teaspoon dried oregano
Salt and pepper to taste

Directions:
1. In a small bowl, soak the breadcrumbs in milk for 5 minutes.
2. Mix all the ingredients in a large bowl, and shape into a loaf.
3. Place the loaf in the Crock Pot.
4. Set the Crock Pot on Low. Cover and cook for 6 hours.

Nutritional Information (Per Serving)
Calories: 390
Fat: 15g
Sat Fat: 4.1g
Carbohydrates: 23g
Fiber: 2g
Sugar: 4g
Protein: 35g
Sodium: 600mg

CHAPTER FIVE

Meats

Spicy Beef Brisket

Servings: 12
Cooking Time: 6 hours
Ingredients:
1 tablespoon olive oil
1 large white onion, sliced
3 garlic cloves, minced
1 (4 pounds) beef brisket
½ teaspoon red pepper flakes, crushed
½ teaspoon paprika
½ teaspoon ground cumin
¼ teaspoon ground cinnamon
Salt and pepper to taste
½ cup beef broth

Directions:
1. In a large Crock Pot, add all ingredients, and mix well.
2. Set the Crock Pot on Low. Cover and cook for about 6 hours.
3. Uncover the Crock Pot, and transfer the brisket onto a cutting board.
4. Set aside for about 10 minutes before slicing.
5. With a sharp knife, cut into desired slices.
6. Serve with a fresh green salad.

Nutritional Information (Per Serving)
Calories: 300
Fat: 10.7g
Sat Fat: 3.8g
Carbohydrates: 1.6g
Fiber: 0g

Sugar: 0.6g
Protein: 46.3g

Herbed Pork with Carrots

Servings: 8
Cooking Time: 8–10 hours
Ingredients:
2 pounds boneless pork shoulder roast
1 teaspoon dried basil, crushed
1 teaspoon dried oregano, crushed
1 teaspoon dried thyme, crushed
1 tablespoon red pepper flakes, crushed
Salt and pepper to taste
1 large onion, sliced thinly
4 medium carrots, peeled and sliced lengthwise

Directions:
1. Rub the pork shoulder generously with dried herbs, salt, and pepper.
2. Arrange the pork in a large bowl, and set aside, covered for at least 3–4 hours.
3. In the bottom of a large Crock Pot, place onion and carrots, and sprinkle with salt and pepper.
4. Place the pork shoulder over the carrots.
5. Set the Crock Pot on Low. Cover and cook for 8–10 hours.

Nutritional Information (Per Serving)
Calories: 354
Fat: 24.4g
Sat Fat: 8.9g
Carbohydrates: 5.3g
Fiber: 1.5g
Sugar: 2.4g
Protein: 27g

Beef Curry

Servings: 4
Cooking Time: 4 hours
Ingredients:
1¼ pounds chuck roast
1 cup water
3 tablespoons coconut milk powder
1½ tablespoons Thai red curry paste
3 pods cardamom, cracked
½ tablespoon dried onion flakes
½ tablespoon ground coriander
A pinch ground nutmeg
1 tablespoon Thai fish sauce
1 tablespoon dried or fresh Thai red chilies
½ tablespoon ground cumin
A pinch ground cloves
½ tablespoon ground ginger

To serve:
1 tablespoon coconut milk powder
2 tablespoons cashew, chopped
½ tablespoon Thai red curry paste
A handful fresh cilantro, chopped

Directions:
1. Add all the ingredients into the Crock Pot and stir.
2. Close the lid. Set the pot on High and cook for 4 hours.
3. Remove the meat with a slotted spoon and place it in a bowl. Chop or break into smaller pieces.
4. Add all the serving ingredients except cilantro into the Crock Pot and mix.
5. Add the meat back into the pot. Mix well.
6. Garnish with cilantro and serve.

Nutritional Information (Per Serving)
Calories: 365

Fat: 17g
Sat Fat: 7.7g
Carbohydrates: 5.8g
Fiber: 0.9g
Sugar: 1.4g
Protein: 44.6g
Sodium: 489mg

Beef and Cabbage Stew

Servings: 6
Cooking Time: 9 hours
Ingredient:
2 pounds beef stew meat, trimmed and cubed
Salt and pepper to taste
5 cups green cabbage, chopped
1 large onion, chopped
4 garlic cloves, minced
4 fresh tomatoes, chopped finely
1 cup beef broth
¼ cup fresh parsley, chopped

Directions:
1. Season the beef generously with salt and pepper.
2. In the bottom of a large Crock Pot, place the cabbage, onion, and garlic.
3. Top with beef, followed by tomatoes. Pour broth on top and stir gently to combine.
4. Set the Crock Pot on Low. Cover and cook for about 9 hours.
5. Serve with a garnish of fresh parsley.

Nutritional Information (Per Serving)
Calories: 452
Fat: 31.8g
Sat Fat: 12.6g
Carbohydrates: 11g
Fiber: 3.2g
Sugar: 0g
Protein: 29.7g

Korean Beef Stew

Servings: 6
Cooking Time: 8–9 hours
Ingredients:
2 pounds beef chuck, cubed
1 medium onion, sliced
4 cloves garlic, minced
1 tablespoon fresh ginger, grated
½ cup soy sauce
¼ cup brown sugar
2 tablespoons Korean red chili paste
2 tablespoons sesame oil
½ teaspoon black pepper
4 cups beef broth
3 medium carrots, peeled and chopped
2 medium potatoes, peeled and cut into 1-inch cubes

Directions:
1. Add all the ingredients into the Crock Pot and stir.
2. Close the lid. Set the pot on Low and cook for 8–9 hours.
3. Serve warm.

Nutritional Information (Per Serving)
Calories: 396
Fat: 16.2g
Sat Fat: 4g
Carbohydrates: 26.1g
Fiber: 3g
Sugar: 10g
Protein: 36g
Sodium: 1396mg

Miraculous Meatloaf

Servings: 6
Cooking Time: 6 hours
Ingredients:
2 pounds ground beef
3 eggs
2/3 cup shredded coconut
½ onion, minced
1 tablespoon fresh sage
1 teaspoon salt
2 tomatoes, diced
1 teaspoon ground mustard

Directions:
1. Place the diced tomatoes in a Crock Pot.
2. Mix all the other ingredients in a large bowl, and shape into a loaf.
3. Place the loaf on top of the tomatoes in the slow cooker.
4. Set the Crock Pot on Low. Cover and cook for 6 hours to ensure no pink is left in the meat.

Nutritional Information (Per Serving)
Calories: 573
Fat: 48.5g
Sat Fat: 22.3g
Carbohydrates: 5.6g
Fiber: 1.9g
Sugar: 0.7g
Protein: 29.1g
Sodium: 540mg

Italian Meatballs

Servings: 4
Cooking Time: 6 hours
Ingredients:
1 pound ground beef
½ onion, chopped
1 celery stalk, minced
¼ cup parmesan cheese
1 egg
1 teaspoon dried basil
1 teaspoon dried oregano
Salt and pepper to taste
4 tomatoes, chopped
1 can (14 ounces) stewed tomatoes

Directions:
1. Make the meatballs by combining beef, onion, celery, cheese, egg, basil, oregano, salt, and pepper. Roll into balls and place on a plate.
2. Pour the stewed tomatoes and fresh tomatoes into the Crock Pot and place meatballs on top.
3. Cook for 6 hours on low heat.

Nutritional Information (Per Serving)
Calories: 291
Fat: 9.8g
Sat Fat: 3.9g
Carbohydrates: 10.8g
Fiber: 2.9g
Sugar: 6.4g
Protein: 39.4g

Hungarian Goulash

Servings: 4
Cooking Time: 8 hours
Ingredients:
1 tablespoon butter
1 tablespoon Hungarian paprika
1 pound beef stew meat, cubed
¼ teaspoon pepper powder or to taste
½ teaspoon salt or to taste
¼ teaspoon caraway seeds
1 bell pepper of any color, chopped
7½ ounces canned diced tomatoes
1 bay leaf
½ cup onion, chopped
1 clove garlic, sliced
1 cup daikon radish, cubed
1 stalk celery, chopped
¾ cup beef broth

Directions:
1. Place a skillet with butter over medium heat. When it melts, add onions and sauté until translucent.
2. Add garlic and sauté for a few seconds until fragrant. Add paprika and sauté for 5–8 seconds.
3. Add beef and cook until brown. Add salt, pepper, and caraway seeds and stir. Transfer into the Crock Pot.
4. Add the rest of the ingredients and stir.
5. Close the lid. Set the pot on Low and cook for 8 hours or on High for 4 hours.
6. You can top it with zucchini noodles to complete a meal.

Nutritional Information (Per Serving)
Calories: 272
Fat: 10.6g
Sat Fat: 4.6g
Carbohydrates: 6.1g
Fiber: 2.1g

Sugar: 3.2g
Protein: 36.3g
Sodium: 583mg

Mississippi Roast

Servings: 4
Cooking Time: 4 hours
Ingredients:
2 pounds beef chuck roast
½ tablespoon dried parsley
½ tablespoon garlic powder
½ tablespoon dried dill
½ tablespoon dried chives
½ tablespoon onion powder
Salt and pepper to taste
8 ounces jarred deli-sliced pepperoncini's, retain the brine
2 tablespoons butter
1 tablespoon better than beef bouillon

Directions:
1. Add the meat into the Crock Pot. Place pepperoncini's over it. Pour ½ cup of retained brine into the pot. Add the rest of the ingredients except butter and stir.
2. Place butter on top of the meat.
3. Close the lid. Set the pot on High and cook for 4 hours or until meat comes off the bone.
4. Remove the meat with a slotted spoon and place it in a bowl. Shred with a pair of forks and add it back into the pot.
5. Stir and serve.

Nutritional Information (Per Serving)
Calories: 500
Fat: 19.9g
Sat Fat: 9g
Carbohydrates: 7.8g
Fiber: 0.2g
Sugar: 2.6g
Protein: 69.9g

Braised Short Ribs

Servings: 8
Cooking Time: 6 hours 10 minutes
Ingredients:
5 pounds beef short ribs
1 can beef broth
1 can dark lager beer
1 onion, sliced
¼ cup molasses
2 tablespoons cider vinegar
1 teaspoon hot sauce
1 teaspoon thyme
Salt to taste

Directions:
1. Put the short ribs in a Crock Pot.
2. Top the meat with beef broth, molasses, onions, hot sauce, cider vinegar, and thyme.
3. Stir to combine the ingredients.
4. Pour the lager into the Crock Pot.
5. Cook for 6 hours on high or 12 hours on low.
6. Use a tong or slotted spoon to place the ribs on a platter.
7. Transfer the gravy into a bowl.
8. Serve the ribs with gravy and mashed potatoes.

Nutritional Information (Per Serving)
Calories: 649
Fat: 26g
Sat Fat: 9.8g
Carbohydrates: 10.9g
Fiber: 0.3g
Sugar: 6.5g
Protein: 83.7g

Cabbage and Ribs

Servings: 4
Cooking Time: 6 hours
Ingredients:
3 pounds beef short ribs (about six ribs)
1 head of green cabbage, quartered
4 green onions, sliced
4 tablespoons soy sauce
4 tablespoons water
½ cup red wine vinegar
2 cloves garlic, minced
1 tablespoon fresh ginger, grated
½ teaspoon red pepper flakes
1 tablespoon sesame oil

Directions:
1. Combine all ingredients in a Crock Pot with the cabbage on top.
2. Cook on High for 6 hours until the meat on the ribs easily pulls away from the bone.

Nutritional Information (Per Serving)
Calories: 752
Fat: 46.3g
Sat Fat: 15.6g
Carbohydrates: 27g
Fiber: 5.2g
Sugar: 11.5g
Protein: 53.8g
Sodium: 1077mg

Barbecue Beef Stew

Servings: 3
Cooking Time: 7 hours 30 minutes
Ingredients:
For barbecue sauce:
3½ ounces tomato paste
½ teaspoon salt
½ teaspoon smoked paprika
6 tablespoons balsamic vinegar
½ teaspoon garlic powder
¼ teaspoon black pepper

For stew:
1 pound beef stew meat, boneless, cubed
¼ teaspoon pepper
½ teaspoon arrowroot starch mixed with 1 tablespoon water
½ teaspoon salt
½ tablespoon olive oil

Directions:
1. Add all the ingredients of barbecue sauce in a bowl and whisk well.
2. Sprinkle salt and pepper over beef.
3. Place a skillet with oil over medium heat. Add beef and cook until brown on all the sides. Transfer into the Crock Pot.
4. Pour sauce into the pot and mix well.
5. Cover, set the pot on Low, and cook for 7 hours.
6. Add arrowroot starch mixture and stir. Cook on High for 20–30 minutes.
7. Serve warm.

Nutritional Information (Per Serving)
Calories: 338
Fat: 12g
Sat Fat: 3.9g
Carbohydrates: 7.4g
Fiber: 1.6g

Sugar: 4.3g
Protein: 47.5g
Sodium: 909mg

Slow Cooker Chili

Servings: 8
Cooking Time: 4 hours
Ingredients:
2 pounds lean ground beef
28-ounce can diced tomatoes
1 red bell pepper, chopped
1 green bell pepper, chopped
¼ red onion, chopped
1 jalapeno pepper, seeded and chopped
½ teaspoon cilantro
Salt to taste

Directions:
1. In a large skillet, cook the ground beef until brown.
2. Pour it into the Crock Pot and add the tomatoes, peppers, and onion.
3. Sprinkle with cilantro and cook on High for 4 hours.
4. Feel free to add or subtract the amount of jalapeno, depending on how spicy you like your chili. You can lighten it up by using ground turkey instead of ground beef if you want less fat.

Nutritional Information (Per Serving)
Calories: 240
Fat: 7.1g
Sat Fat: 2.7g
Carbohydrates: 7g
Fiber: 2.3g
Sugar: 4.6g
Protein: 35.6g

Paprika Pork

Servings: 4
Cooking Time: 8 hours
Ingredients:
1¼ pounds pork tenderloin
2 tablespoons butter, melt
2 cloves garlic, minced
½ tablespoon paprika
½ tablespoon Worcestershire sauce
2 tablespoons chicken broth
A handful fresh thyme, chopped
½ cup onion, chopped
1 small red bell pepper, diced
¼ teaspoon ground caraway
4 teaspoons red wine vinegar
2 tablespoons tomato paste
½ cup sour cream
Salt and pepper to taste

Directions:
1. Sprinkle salt and pepper over the pork, brush with butter, and place in the Crock Pot.
2. Add onion, garlic, pepper, and thyme.
3. Add the rest of the ingredients except sour cream into a bowl. Mix well and pour over the pork.
4. Close the lid. Set the pot on Low and cook for 8 hours.
5. Remove the pork with a slotted spoon and place it on your cutting board. When cool enough to handle, shred the pork with a pair of forks.
6. Add the pork back into the pot. Stir well.
7. Cook for 10 minutes without the lid.
8. Add sour cream. Stir and serve.

Nutritional Information (Per Serving)
Calories: 347
Fat: 17.1g

Sat Fat: 9.2g
Carbohydrates: 7.9g
Fiber: 1.5g
Sugar: 3.7g
Protein: 39.5g

Doughless Pizza

Servings: 8
Cooking Time: 4 hours
Ingredients:
1 28-ounce can whole tomatoes
1 6-ounce can tomato paste
1 pound Italian sausage
½ stick pepperoni, sliced
1 cup black olives
1 red onion, sliced
1 cup mushrooms, chopped
1 green bell pepper, chopped
3 cloves garlic, minced
½ cup water
4 sprigs thyme, chopped
6 fresh basil leaves, chopped

Directions:

1. Remove sausage from casing, and cook in a skillet until brown.
2. Place the sausage and all the other ingredients into the Crock Pot, and stir until everything is combined.
3. Cook on High for 4 hours.
4. Feel free to customize this recipe to add all your favorite pizza toppings.

Nutritional Information (Per Serving)
Calories: 569
Fat: 51.3g
Sat Fat: 12.4g
Carbohydrates: 12.0g
Fiber: 2.8g
Sugar: 5.4g
Protein: 16.7g
Sodium: 1,311mg

Pork Burgers

Servings: 12
Cooking Time: 10 hours
Ingredients:
For Pork:
1 teaspoon dried oregano, crushed
1 teaspoon ground cumin
½ teaspoon ground coriander
½ teaspoon garlic powder
¼ teaspoon ground cinnamon
Salt and pepper to taste
1 (4 pounds) boneless pork shoulder roast
2 bay leaves
2 cups chicken broth

For Burgers:
12 whole-wheat hamburger buns, split
1 cup ketchup
2 cups lettuce, shredded
12 tomato slices
1 onion, sliced

Directions:
1. In a bowl, mix oregano, spices, salt, and pepper.
2. Rub the pork roast generously with the spice mixture.
3. In the bottom of a Crock Pot, place bay leaves and top with pork roast. Pour broth on top.
4. Set the Crock Pot on Low. Cover and cook for about 5 hours.
5. Uncover the Crock Pot, and flip over the pork roast. Cover and cook for about another 5 hours.
6. Uncover the Crock Pot, and with 2 forks, shred the pork roast.
7. Discard the bay leaves from the Crock Pot.
8. Mix the shredded pork with pan juices.
9. For burgers, spread ketchup evenly over the inside of each burger bun.

10. Divide lettuce, followed by shredded pork, tomato, and onion slices.

11. Serve immediately.

Nutritional Information (Per Serving)
Calories: 537
Fat: 34.4g
Sat Fat: 12.3g
Carbohydrates: 25.7g
Fiber: 3.4g
Sugar: 8.6g
Protein: 39.8g
Sodium: 583mg

Country Style Pork Ribs

Servings: 4
Cooking Time: 7–8 hours
Ingredients:
2½ pounds short pork ribs
Salt and pepper to taste
1 tablespoon olive oil
1 small onion, sliced
3 cloves garlic, minced
1 cup barbecue sauce
½ cup apple cider vinegar
½ cup beef broth
1 teaspoon smoked paprika
1 teaspoon dried thyme

Directions:
1. Add all the ingredients into the Crock Pot and stir.
2. Close the lid. Set the pot on Low and cook for 7–8 hours.
3. Serve warm.

Nutritional Information (Per Serving)
Calories: 797
Fat: 54g
Sat Fat: 17g
Carbohydrates: 36g
Fiber: 2.1g
Sugar: 27g
Protein: 42g

Pulled Pork

Servings: 8
Cooking Time: 8–10 hours
Ingredients:
4 pounds pork shoulder
1 tablespoon olive oil
1 cup barbecue sauce
½ cup apple cider vinegar
½ cup chicken broth
¼ cup brown sugar
1 tablespoon smoked paprika
1 tablespoon chili powder
1 teaspoon salt
1 teaspoon black pepper
1 small onion, thinly sliced
3 cloves garlic, minced

Directions:
1. Add all the ingredients into the Crock Pot and stir.
2. Close the lid. Set the pot on Low and cook for 8–10 hours.
3. Use two forks to shred the pork.
4. Serve warm.

Nutritional Information (Per Serving)
Calories: 474
Fat: 27g
Sat Fat: 8.0g
Carbohydrates: 20g
Fiber: 0.9g
Sugar: 15g
Protein: 37g
Sodium: 914mg

Pork Chops with Spice Rub

Servings: 4
Cooking Time: 4 hours
Ingredients:
1 pound pork chops
½ tablespoons dried rosemary
½ tablespoon curry powder
½ tablespoon fennel seeds
½ teaspoon salt
½ tablespoon dried thyme
½ tablespoon fresh chives, chopped
½ tablespoon ground cumin
2 tablespoons olive oil
½ cup beef broth

Directions:
1. Pour half the oil into the Crock Pot.
2. In a bowl, mix the rest of the ingredients except the pork chops and broth, and rub it all over the chops.
3. Add broth to the pot, place the chops in it, and close the lid.
4. Set the pot on High and cook for 4 hours.

Nutritional Information (Per Serving)
Calories: 438
Fat: 35.8g
Sat Fat: 11.7g
Carbohydrates: 1.8g
Fiber: 0.9g
Sugar: 0.2g
Protein: 26.5g
Sodium: 468mg

Roasted Leg of Lamb

Servings: 10
Cooking Time: 8 hours
Ingredients:
2 tablespoons olive oil
5 garlic cloves, minced
1 tablespoon fresh rosemary, minced
1 tablespoon fresh thyme, minced
2 teaspoons lemon zest, grated
1 teaspoon red pepper flakes, crushed
1 teaspoon cayenne pepper
½ teaspoon ground cumin
Salt and pepper to taste
1 (3 lb.) boneless leg of lamb
½ cup chicken broth
2 tablespoons fresh lemon juice

Directions:
1. In a bowl, add oil, garlic, herbs, lemon zest, and spices, and mix until well combined.
2. Rub the lamb generously with the oil mixture.
3. In a large Crock Pot, place the lamb leg. Pour broth and lemon juice evenly on top.
4. Set the Crock Pot on Low. Cover and cook for about 8 hours.

Nutritional Information (Per Serving)
Calories: 286
Fat: 13g
Sat Fat: 9.5g
Carbohydrates: 1.3g
Fiber: 0g
Sugar: 0g
Protein: 38.7g

Mustard Rosemary Lamb

Servings: 6
Cooking Time: 8 hours
Ingredients:
3 pounds leg of lamb
3 tablespoons whole-grain mustard
6 sprigs thyme
1¼ teaspoons dried rosemary
Salt and pepper to taste
2 tablespoons olive oil
½ cup beef broth
A handful of fresh mint leaves
1½ teaspoons garlic, minced

Directions:
1. Score the lamb at 4–5 places. Place garlic and rosemary in the slits.
2. Place in the Crock Pot. Rub oil over it. Sprinkle mustard, salt, and pepper over it and rub it well.
3. Add the broth and close the lid.
4. Set the pot on Low and cook for 8 hours. Add thyme and mint during the last hour of cooking.

Nutritional Information (Per Serving)
Calories: 371
Fat: 16.4g
Sat Fat: 4.8g
Carbohydrates: 2.5g
Fiber: 1g
Sugar: 0.5g
Protein: 47.9g

Balsamic Lamb Leg

Servings: 2
Cooking Time: 8 hours
Ingredients:
2 pounds lamb leg
1 sprig fresh rosemary
Salt to taste
3 tablespoons balsamic vinegar
2 cloves garlic, minced
1 head lettuce
1 cup water

Directions:
1. Place lamb in the Crock Pot.
2. Add the rest of the ingredients except lettuce into a bowl and mix well. Pour over the lamb.
3. Close the lid. Set the pot on Low and cook for 8 hours or on High for 4 hours.
4. Remove the lamb with a slotted spoon and place it on your cutting board. When cool enough to handle, shred the lamb with a pair of forks.
5. Add the lamb back into the pot. Stir well. Cook for 10 minutes without the lid.
6. Place the lettuce leaves on a serving platter. Spoon the lamb on it and serve.

Nutritional Information (Per Serving)
Calories: 632
Fat: 20.4g
Sat Fat: 8g
Carbohydrates: 6.2g
Fiber: 1.2g
Sugar: 1.7g
Protein: 93g

Braised Lamb

Servings: 4
Cooking Time: 6 hours
Ingredients:
4 lamb shanks (keep the fat on)
1 Vidalia onion, diced
2 carrots, peeled and chopped
2 stalks of celery, chopped
3 garlic cloves, chopped
2 tomatoes, chopped
2 cups beef stock
2 tablespoons of olive oil
1 cup red wine
1 bay leaf
1 teaspoon fresh thyme, chopped
Salt and pepper to taste

Directions:
1. Season the lamb with salt and pepper, and cook in the olive oil in a large pan over medium-high heat. Cook for five minutes on each side until the outsides are brown.
2. Meanwhile, place the onion, carrots, celery, garlic, tomatoes, thyme, and bay leaf into the Crock Pot. Place the cooked lamb on top of the vegetables in the pot.
3. Take the frying pan off the heat. Add the wine and simmer, scraping the bits of cooked lamb off the bottom of the frying pan. Add the drippings to the slow cooker.
4. Cook on High for 6 hours.

Nutritional Information (Per Serving)
Calories: 557
Fat: 26.5g
Sat Fat: 8.2g
Carbohydrates: 29.8g
Fiber: 6.4g
Sugar: 10.9g
Protein: 35.7g

Moroccan Lamb Stew

Servings: 6
Cooking Time: 8 hours
Ingredients:
2 pounds lamb, cut into chunks
2 large sweet potatoes, diced
1 green pepper, chopped
4 tablespoons Ras El Hanout Spice Blend
1 cup dried apricots, diced
2 tomatoes, chopped
3 tablespoons butter
2 cups coconut milk
Salt to taste

Directions:
1. Heat a sauce pan over medium heat and roast the spice blend. Add the lamb and mix well with the spice blend.
2. Add the butter to sear the lamb, then transfer it to a Crock Pot.
3. Add the rest of the ingredients, and cook on Low for 8 hours.
4. Serve with your favorite vegetable.

Nutritional Information (Per Serving)
Calories: 583
Fat: 36.2g
Sat Fat: 24.6g
Carbohydrates: 20.8g
Fiber: 4.4g
Sugar: 8.9g
Protein: 46.1g

Venison Steak and Veggies

Servings: 4
Cooking Time: 6 hours
Ingredients:
4 venison steaks, 8 ounces each
1 onion, chopped
1 eggplant, chopped
2 carrots, chopped
3 cloves garlic, chopped
Salt and pepper to taste
1 cup red wine

Directions:
1. Season venison with salt and pepper and place in the Crock Pot.
2. Top with onion, eggplant, carrots, and garlic.
3. Pour red wine over the ingredients and cook on Low for 6 hours or on High for 3 hours.

Nutritional Information (Per Serving)
Calories: 346
Fat: 2.5g
Sat Fat: 0g
Carbohydrates: 14.6g
Fiber: 5.4g
Sugar: 6.6g
Protein: 51.1g

CHAPTER SIX

Fish and Seafood

Lemon Tuna Steaks

Servings: 4
Cooking Time: 1–2 hours
Ingredients:
4 tuna steaks
¼ cup soy sauce
2 tablespoons olive oil
2 tablespoons lemon juice
1 tablespoon honey
2 garlic cloves, minced
1 tablespoon fresh ginger, grated
2 green onions, chopped
Salt and pepper to taste

Directions:
1. In a Crock Pot, mix all ingredients except tuna steaks and green onions.
2. Place tuna steaks in the Crock Pot.
3. Close the lid. Set the pot on High and cook for 1–2 hours.
4. Garnish with chopped green onions and serve.

Nutritional Information (Per Serving)
Calories: 289
Fat: 9.2g
Sat Fat: 1.0g
Carbohydrates: 10g
Fiber: 0g
Sugar: 8g
Protein: 13g
Sodium: 590mg

Seafood Stew

Servings: 6
Cooking Time: 6 hours 45 minutes
Ingredients:
28 ounces crushed tomatoes
3 cups vegetable broth
1½ cups white wine
3 minced garlic cloves
1 pound potatoes, cut into chunks
½ cup onion, diced
1 teaspoon basil
1 teaspoon thyme
¼ teaspoon red pepper flakes
⅛ teaspoon cayenne pepper
Salt and pepper to taste
2 pounds seafood (shrimp, crab legs, or firm whitefish)

Directions:
1. Place all ingredients, except for the seafood, in the Crock Pot and stir.
2. Cook on Low for 6 hours. Make sure the potatoes are done.
3. Add the seafood, and set the temperature to High.
4. Cook for another 45 minutes, but check on the seafood after 30 minutes. You don't want to overcook.

Nutritional Information (Per Serving)
Calories: 490
Fat: 3.4g
Sat Fat: 1g
Carbohydrates: 32.7g
Fiber: 6.4g
Sugar: 10.8g
Protein: 41.7g

Salmon with Wine Sauce

Servings: 6
Cooking Time: 1–2 hours
Ingredients:
1 cup dry white wine
1½ cups water
1 shallot, sliced thinly
1 lemon, sliced thinly
¼ cup fresh dill, chopped finely
Salt and pepper to taste
6 (4 ounces) salmon fillets

Directions:
1. In a Crock Pot, mix all ingredients except salmon fillets.
2. Place salmon fillets on top, skin side down.
3. Set the Crock Pot on Low. Cover and cook for 1–2 hours.

Nutritional Information (Per Serving)
Calories: 192
Fat: 7.1g
Sat Fat: 1g
Carbohydrates: 3.4g
Fiber: 0g
Sugar: 0g
Protein: 22.6g

Indonesian Fish

Servings: 6
Cooking Time: 5 hours
Ingredients:
1 large onion, sliced
4 tablespoons fresh lime juice
3 pounds fish steak (use halibut or swordfish)
3 tablespoons soy sauce
Salt to taste
Crushed red pepper flakes to taste
2 tablespoons olive oil
½ teaspoon ground pepper
1 teaspoon ground coriander

Directions:
1. Add half the onions, soy sauce, lime juice, coriander, crushed red pepper, salt, pepper, and olive oil into a bowl and mix well. Place the fish pieces in it. Turn the fish so that it is well coated.
2. Sprinkle the rest of the onions over the fish. Cover the bowl with cling wrap.
3. Place the bowl in the refrigerator for 3–4 hours.
4. Transfer the ingredients to the Crock Pot.
5. Close the lid. Set the pot on High and cook for 2 hours.
6. Transfer to a serving platter. Pour the cooking liquid over the fish and serve.

Nutritional Information (Per Serving)
Calories: 208
Fat: 12.7g
Sat Fat: 2.7g
Carbohydrates: 4.3g
Fiber: 0.7g
Sugar: 1.5g
Protein: 19.9g

Poached Salmon

Servings: 8
Cooking Time: 1 hour 30 minutes
Ingredients:
4 cups water
2 bay leaves
2 teaspoons black peppercorns
8 salmon fillets
4 sprigs rosemary
2 cloves garlic, minced
2 teaspoons kosher salt
Freshly ground pepper and salt to taste
2 lemons, thinly sliced

To serve:
Lemon wedges
Olive oil
Coarse sea salt

Directions:
1. Add water, bay leaves, black peppercorns, rosemary, and garlic into the pot.
2. Close the lid. Set the pot on High and cook for 30 minutes.
3. Sprinkle salt and pepper over the salmon and place in the Crock Pot.
4. Set the pot on High and cook for 1 hour. Keep a check on the salmon after 45 minutes of cooking. Cook until done.
5. Remove the salmon with a slotted spoon and place it on a serving platter.
6. Sprinkle with sea salt and drizzle oil, and serve with lemon wedges.

Nutritional Information (Per Serving)
Calories: 242
Fat: 11.1g
Sat Fat: 1.6g

Carbohydrates: 2g
Fiber: 0.6g
Sugar: 0.4g
Protein: 34.8g

Citrus Salmon

Servings: 4
Cooking Time: 1 hour 30 minutes
Ingredients:
2 pounds wild salmon with skin
2 cups water
1 cup freshly squeezed orange juice
1 lemon, sliced thin
1 shallot, sliced
1 bay leaf
6 sprigs fresh Italian parsley
1 teaspoon black pepper
1 teaspoon sea salt
¼ cup olive oil

Directions:
1. Combine water, orange juice, lemons, shallot, bay leaf, and parsley in the Crock Pot and heat on High for 30 minutes.

2. Sprinkle salt and pepper on salmon and place in the pot, skin side down. Drizzle with olive oil.

3. Cook on Low for 1 hour.

Nutritional Information (Per Serving)
Calories: 408
Fat: 20.6g
Sat Fat: 3.1g
Carbohydrates: 8.7g
Fiber: 0.7g
Sugar: 5.6g
Protein: 46.1g
Sodium: 623mg

Spicy Mussels

Servings: 4
Cooking Time: 2–3 hours
Ingredients:
2 pounds fresh mussels, cleaned and de-bearded
1 can (14.5 ounces) diced tomatoes with green chilies
1 cup white wine
1 small onion, chopped
4 garlic cloves, minced
1 red chili pepper, chopped (adjust to taste)
1 teaspoon smoked paprika
1 teaspoon dried oregano
½ teaspoon black pepper
½ teaspoon salt
2 tablespoons olive oil
Fresh parsley, chopped for garnish

Directions:
1. Place all ingredients, except for the parsley, in the Crock Pot and stir.
2. Close the lid. Set the pot on High and cook for 2–3 hours.
3. Garnish with fresh parsley and serve immediately. Discard any mussels that have not opened after cooking.

Nutritional Information (Per Serving)
Calories: 364
Fat: 14g
Sat Fat: 1.9g
Carbohydrates: 19g
Fiber: 3.8g
Sugar: 7.1g
Protein: 26g
Sodium: 965mg

Shrimp Scampi

Servings: 3
Cooking Time: 2 hours 40 minutes
Ingredients:
¼ cup chicken broth
½ cup vermouth
3 diced garlic cloves
2 tablespoons olive oil
1 teaspoon chopped parsley
1 pound raw shrimp

Directions:
1. Place all ingredients in the Crock Pot and stir.
2. Cook for 2½ hours on Low or 1½ hours on High.
3. Use a tong or slotted spoon to transfer the shrimp to individual plates or bowls.
4. Spoon the broth over the shrimp.

Nutritional Information (Per Serving)
Calories: 310
Fat: 12g
Sat Fat: 2.1g
Carbohydrates: 3.7g
Fiber: 0.1g
Sugar: 0.1g
Protein: 35g
Sodium: 436mg

Polenta with Shrimp

Servings: 6
Cooking Time: 8 hours
Ingredients:
For Polenta:
2 cups cornmeal
4 cups water
4 cups milk
Salt to taste
½ cup shredded Cheddar cheese

For Shrimp:
1 lb. uncooked peeled and deveined shrimp without tails
¼ cup olive oil
2 tablespoons lemon juice
2 minced garlic cloves
Salt and pepper to taste
If you like extra heat, add 1 teaspoon chili powder

Directions:
1. Add the cornmeal to the Crock Pot.
2. Pour the water and milk into a pan, and bring to a boil.
3. Pour the hot liquid over the cornmeal.
4. Stir in the salt, and combine well.
5. Cook for 8 hours on Low or 4 hours on High.
6. Add the shredded cheese, and stir until it melts. Turn off the slow cooker, but keep the polenta warm.
7. Combine all the shrimp ingredients in a bowl and combine.
8. Refrigerate the shrimp for 15 minutes.
9. Add the shrimp to a skillet, and brown on each side for 4 minutes.
10. Transfer the polenta to a plate, and top with the shrimp.

Nutritional Information (Per Serving)
Calories: 430
Fat: 17.6g
Sat Fat: 5.8g

Carbohydrates: 40.9g
Fiber: 3g
Sugar: 7.7 g
Protein: 28.3g
Sodium: 339mg

Spicy Shrimp

Servings: 4
Cooking Time: 4 hours
Ingredients:
1 pound shrimp, shelled and deveined
2 stalks celery, diced
1 small onion, chopped
1 red bell pepper, chopped
28 ounces diced tomatoes
1 clove garlic, minced
¼ teaspoon black pepper
¼ teaspoon white pepper
½ teaspoon red pepper flakes
5 drops of Tabasco sauce
Salt to taste

Directions:
1. Combine all ingredients in the Crock Pot except for the shrimp.
2. Cook for 3 hours on High and stir all the ingredients together.
3. Add shrimp and cook for 1 more hour. If you're looking for something hot to go with a salad, this makes an excellent pairing. If shrimp is not your favorite seafood, you can substitute it for other types of fish.

Nutritional Information (Per Serving)
Calories: 191
Fat: 2.5g
Sat Fat: 0.7g
Carbohydrates: 14.1g
Fiber: 3.5g
Sugar: 7.6g
Protein: 28.2g

Lemon Pepper Tilapia with Asparagus

Servings: 8
Cooking Time: 3 hours
Ingredients:
8 tilapia fillets
20 asparagus spears, chopped
8 teaspoons lemon-pepper seasoning or to taste
4 tablespoons butter
½ cup lemon juice

Directions:
1. Take 8 foils. Lay the fillets in the middle of the foil. Sprinkle 1 teaspoon lemon pepper seasoning over it.
2. Place ½ tablespoon of butter on each of the fillets. Divide and place asparagus over the fish.
3. Wrap foil all around the fish. Seal it well.
4. Place the packets in the Crock Pot. It can be overlapped while placing it.
5. Close the lid. Set the pot on High and cook for 2 hours if thawed and 3 hours if frozen.

Nutritional Information (Per Serving)
Calories: 182
Fat: 8.5g
Sat Fat: 4.8g
Carbohydrates: 4g
Fiber: 1.9g
Sugar: 1.5g
Protein: 23.7g
Sodium: 376mg

Fish Curry

Servings: 8
Cooking Time: 4 hours
Ingredients:
2 tablespoons ginger, minced
3 tablespoons curry powder
3 tablespoons olive oil
1 teaspoon ground cinnamon
4 cloves garlic, minced
1 teaspoon turmeric powder
1 teaspoon chili powder
1 bell pepper, finely chopped
1 chili pepper, chopped
2 tomatoes, chopped
1 cup water
3 pounds tilapia, cubed
Salt to taste

Directions:
1. Add all the ingredients except tilapia into the Crock Pot and stir.
2. Close the lid. Set the pot on Low and cook for 4 hours. Add tilapia during the last 45 minutes of cooking time.
3. Stir and serve.

Nutritional Information (Per Serving)
Calories: 213
Fat: 7.4g
Sat Fat: 1.5g
Carbohydrates: 5.8g
Fiber: 1.9g
Sugar: 1.8g
Protein: 32.7g

Lemon Herbed Tilapia

Servings: 6
Cooking Time: 1½ hours
Ingredients:
6 (4 oz.) skinless tilapia fillets
Salt and pepper to taste
½ cup onion, chopped
2 teaspoons fresh lemon rind, grated
2 tablespoons fresh parsley, chopped
2 tablespoons fresh dill, chopped
2 tablespoons unsalted butter, melted
1 lemon, cut into wedges

Directions:
1. Grease a Crock Pot with butter-flavored cooking spray.
2. Sprinkle the tilapia fillets generously with salt and pepper.
3. Arrange the tilapia fillets in the bottom of the Crock Pot.
4. Place onion, lemon rind, and parsley evenly over fillets. Drizzle with melted butter.
5. Set the Crock Pot on High. Cover and cook for about 1½ hours.
6. Serve these fillets with lemon slices.

Nutritional Information (Per Serving)
Calories: 153
Fat: 5.9g
Sat Fat: 2.9g
Carbohydrates: 3.2g
Fiber: 1.1g
Sugar: 0g
Protein: 24.5g

Chinese-Style Salmon

Servings: 4
Cooking Time: 3 hours
Ingredients:
4 10-oz. salmon fillets
2 cups frozen mixed Asian vegetables
Salt and pepper to taste
2 tablespoons soy sauce
2 tablespoons honey
1½ tablespoons lemon juice

Directions:
1. Place the vegetables inside the Crock Pot.
2. Salt and pepper the salmon fillets.
3. Lay the salmon on top of the vegetables.
4. Stir the remaining ingredients together in a bowl, and pour on the salmon.
5. Cook for 3 hours on High.
6. Serve with white rice. Drizzle the cooking juices over the salmon.

Nutritional Information (Per Serving)
Calories: 441
Fat: 17.7g
Sat Fat: 2.7g
Carbohydrates: 15.2g
Fiber: 1.2g
Sugar: 10.7g
Protein: 56.7g
Sodium: 591mg

Spicy Seafood Stew

Servings: 2
Cooking Time: 6 hours
Ingredients:
½ cup chicken broth
1 small bell pepper, chopped
1 small onion, chopped
7 ounces canned diced tomatoes
1 clove garlic, minced
4 ounces tomato sauce
Hot pepper sauce to taste
½ cup water
1 bay leaf
2 tablespoons olive oil
¼ teaspoon Cajun seasoning
1½ teaspoons dried thyme
3 ounces shrimp, peeled, deveined
4 ounces fish fillets, skinless, cut into 1-inch pieces
A handful fresh parsley, chopped, to garnish

Directions:
1. Add all the ingredients except seafood to the Crock Pot. Mix well.
2. Close the lid. Set the pot on Low and cook for 6 hours or on High for 3 hours.
3. Add the seafood during the last 30 minutes of cooking and stir.
4. Stir occasionally while it is cooking.
5. Ladle into soup bowls. Garnish with parsley and serve.

Nutritional Information (Per Serving)
Calories: 394
Fat: 22.7g
Sat Fat: 4g
Carbohydrates: 28g
Fiber: 6g
Sugar: 9.7g

Protein: 22.8g
Sodium: 919mg

Lemon Pepper Cod with Asparagus

Servings: 4
Cooking Time: 2 hours
Ingredients:
1 pound fresh cod filets
1 bundle of asparagus
2 lemons
4 teaspoons black pepper, divided
4 teaspoons white pepper, divided
4 tablespoons butter, divided.

Directions:
1. Place each fish filet on a piece of foil. Cover with asparagus. Sprinkle with peppers and then squeeze the juice from half a lemon onto each fish filet.
2. Add one tablespoon of butter to each piece of fish and then wrap the foil around the fish until it is completely sealed.
3. Place the 4 packets in the Crock Pot.
4. Cook on High for 2 hours.

Nutritional Information (Per Serving)
Calories: 226
Fat: 12.8g
Sat Fat: 7.4g
Carbohydrates: 8g
Fiber: 3.3g
Sugar: 2g
Protein: 22.6g
Sodium: 157mg

CHAPTER SEVEN

Soups

Cauliflower and Ham Soup

Servings: 5
Cooking Time: 4½ hours
Ingredients:
12 ounces cauliflower florets
1 cup water
3 cups chicken broth
½ teaspoon onion powder
¼ teaspoon garlic powder
1½ cups ham, chopped
2 teaspoons fresh thyme leaves, chopped
1 tablespoon apple cider vinegar
1 tablespoon butter
Salt and pepper to taste

Directions:
1. Add cauliflower, onion powder, garlic powder, water, and broth into the Crock Pot.
2. Close the lid. Set the pot on Low and cook for 4 hours or until cauliflower is soft.
3. Blend with an immersion blender until smooth.
4. Add ham and thyme leaves. Cover and cook on High for 30 minutes.
5. Add butter, salt, pepper, and apple cider vinegar and stir.
6. Ladle into soup bowls and serve.

Nutritional Information (Per Serving)
Calories: 129
Fat: 6.7g

Sat Fat: 2.9g
Carbohydrates: 6.3g
Fiber: 2.4g
Sugar: 2.2g
Protein: 11.1g

Vegetable Chickpea Soup

Servings: 6
Cooking Time: 6–8 hours
Ingredients:
2 cans (15 ounces each) chickpeas, drained and rinsed
1 large onion, diced
3 carrots, peeled and sliced
3 celery stalks, chopped
3 garlic cloves, minced
1 bell pepper, diced
1 can (14.5 ounces) diced tomatoes, with juice
6 cups vegetable broth
2 teaspoons ground cumin
1 teaspoon dried oregano
½ teaspoon smoked paprika
½ teaspoon turmeric
Salt and pepper to taste
2 tablespoons olive oil

Directions:
1. Add all the ingredients into the Crock Pot and stir.
2. Close the lid. Set the pot on Low and cook for 6–8 hours.
3. Serve warm.

Nutritional Information (Per Serving)
Calories: 220
Fat: 6.1g
Sat Fat: 0.9g
Carbohydrates: 35g
Fiber: 9.1g
Sugar: 8g
Protein: 7.8g

Kale Chicken Soup

Servings: 4
Cooking Time: 6 hours
Ingredients:
1 pound chicken thighs
1 sprig fresh thyme
1 tablespoon fresh thyme, chopped
Salt and pepper to taste
1 clove garlic, minced
2½ cups chicken broth
1 tablespoon olive oil
1 medium onion, chopped
2 cups packed kale, discard hard stems and ribs, chopped

Directions:
1. Sprinkle salt and pepper over the chicken and place in the Crock Pot.
2. Sprinkle garlic over the chicken. Add chicken broth, oil, and thyme sprig and stir.
3. Close the lid. Set the pot on High and cook for 4 hours. Remove the chicken with a slotted spoon and place it on your cutting board. When cool enough to handle, shred with a pair of forks. Discard the thyme.
4. Add the bones back into the Crock Pot. Refrigerate the chicken.
5. Add the rest of the ingredients.
6. Cover and cook on High for 2 hours.
7. Discard the bones and add chicken into the pot during the last 10 minutes of cooking.
8. Ladle into soup bowls and serve.

Nutritional Information (Per Serving)
Calories: 300
Fat: 12.8g
Sat Fat: 3.1g
Carbohydrates: 7.4g
Fiber: 1.4g

Sugar: 1.6g
Protein: 37.3g

Jalapeño Popper Soup

Servings: 6
Cooking Time: 3 hours
Ingredients:
1½ tablespoons butter
1 small onion, chopped
1–2 jalapeños, deseed if desired, chopped
½ small green pepper, chopped
Salt and pepper to taste
¾ pound chicken breast, skinless, boneless
1½ cups chicken broth
1 large clove garlic, minced
¼ pound bacon, cooked until crisp, crumbled
¼ teaspoon paprika
6 tablespoons cheddar cheese, shredded
6 tablespoons Monterrey Jack cheese, shredded
3 ounces cream cheese
¼ cup heavy whipping cream
½ teaspoon ground cumin

Directions:
1. Place a saucepan with butter over medium heat. Add onion, jalapeño, green pepper, salt, and pepper. Sauté for 2–3 minutes and transfer into the Crock Pot.
2. Add chicken and broth.
3. Close the lid. Set the pot on High and cook for 3 hours.
4. When done, remove the chicken with a slotted spoon and place it on your cutting board. Shred chicken with a fork and add it back into the pot.
5. Add the rest of the ingredients and stir until the cheese melts.
6. Ladle into soup bowls and serve.

Nutritional Information (Per Serving)
Calories: 334
Fat: 24.1g
Sat Fat: 11.8g

Carbohydrates: 3g
Fiber: 0.5g
Sugar: 1g
Protein: 25.2g

Cabbage Roll Soup

Servings: 6
Cooking Time: 3 hours
Ingredients:
2 tablespoons olive oil
¼ cup onion, chopped
2 shallots, chopped
1¼ pounds ground beef
½ teaspoon salt
2 cloves garlic, minced
½ teaspoon dried oregano
½ teaspoon dried parsley
½ teaspoon pepper powder
12 ounces marinara sauce
1 cup cauliflower, grated to a rice-like texture
3 cups beef broth
6 cups cabbage, thinly sliced

Directions:
1. Add oil into a saucepan and place over medium heat.
2. Add onions and shallots and sauté until translucent.
3. Stir in ground beef. Sauté until it is brown.
4. Add spices, salt, and dried herbs. Sauté for a few seconds until fragrant. Transfer into the Crock Pot.
5. Add marinara sauce and mix well. Add cauliflower and stir until well combined.
6. Add beef broth and cabbage and stir well.
7. Close the lid. Set the pot on High and cook for 3 hours.
8. Ladle into soup bowls and serve.

Nutritional Information (Per Serving)
Calories: 313
Fat: 12.9g
Sat Fat: 3.5g
Carbohydrates: 14.8g
Fiber: 3.9g
Sugar: 8.2g

Protein: 33.7g
Sodium: 889mg

Vegetable Soup

Servings: 10
Cooking Time: 6 hours
Ingredients:
2 large sweet potatoes, peeled and diced
2 pounds carrots, peeled and diced
2 red onions, chopped
1 head of garlic, peeled
20 ounces spinach, fresh and rinsed
1 pound frozen peas, thawed
2 cups chicken or beef stock
Salt and pepper to taste

Directions:
1. Place the vegetables into the crock pot and cover with the stock.
2. Sprinkle some salt and pepper on top, then add more later if necessary.
3. Cook on Low for 6 hours. This chunky soup can be pureed after it cooks if you prefer something smoother.

Nutritional Information (Per Serving)
Calories: 151
Fat: 0.6g
Sat Fat: 0.1g
Carbohydrates: 32.5g
Fiber: 8.3g
Sugar: 8.1g
Protein: 5.8g

Beef Cabbage Soup

Servings: 8
Cooking Time: 7–8 hours
Ingredients:
1 pound beef stew meat, cut into bite-sized pieces
1 small head of cabbage, chopped into chunks
1 large onion, diced
3 carrots, peeled and sliced
3 celery stalks, chopped
4 cloves garlic, minced
1 can (14.5 oz) diced tomatoes, with juice
1 can (8 oz) tomato sauce
6 cups beef broth
1 teaspoon paprika
1 teaspoon dried thyme
½ teaspoon black pepper
Salt to taste
2 tablespoons olive oil

Directions:
1. In a skillet, heat the olive oil over medium heat. Add the beef and cook until browned on all sides. Transfer the beef to the Crock Pot.
2. Add all the remaining ingredients and stir.
3. Close the lid. Set the pot on Low and cook for 7–8 hours.
4. Serve warm.

Nutritional Information (Per Serving)
Calories: 189
Fat: 7.1g
Sat Fat: 2.0g
Carbohydrates: 16g
Fiber: 3.9g
Sugar: 7.2g
Protein: 16g

Beef Bone Broth

Servings: 6
Cooking Time: 10 hours
Ingredients:
4 pounds beef bones
2 carrots, chopped
6 cloves garlic, minced
2 stalks of celery, chopped
2 bay leaves
1 teaspoon salt
2 teaspoons apple cider vinegar

Directions:
1. Place the vegetables in the Crock Pot, followed by the beef bones and bay leaves.
2. Add the salt, vinegar, and enough water just to cover the bones.
3. Cook on Low for 10 hours.
4. Discard the bones before serving the soup.

Nutritional Information (Per Serving)
Calories: 20
Fat: 0.2g
Sat Fat: 0.1g
Carbohydrates: 3.2g
Fiber: 0.7g
Sugar: 1.1g
Protein: 1.3g
Sodium: 668mg

Pizza Soup

Servings: 4
Cooking Time: 6–7 hours
Ingredients:
½ pound Italian sausage
8 ounces canned crushed tomatoes
1 can (16 ounces) mushrooms or an equal amount of fresh mushrooms
1 small onion, chopped
¼ pound pepperoni, thinly sliced
1 teaspoon dried oregano
1 cup beef broth
1 small green pepper, chopped
½ teaspoon garlic powder
1 teaspoon Italian seasoning
4 tablespoons mozzarella cheese, freshly grated
2 tablespoons Parmesan cheese, grated

Directions:
1. Place a skillet with sausage over medium heat. Cook until brown. Drain excess fat and transfer sausage into the Crock Pot.
2. Add the rest of the ingredients except both cheese and stir.
3. Close the lid. Set the pot on Low and cook for 6–7 hours.
4. Ladle into soup bowls. Garnish with both the cheese and serve.

Nutritional Information (Per Serving)
Calories: 480
Fat: 35g
Sat Fat: 13g
Carbohydrates: 11g
Fiber: 3.6g
Sugar: 5.5g
Protein: 30.1g
Sodium: 1557mg

Taco Soup

Servings: 4
Cooking Time: 6 hours
Ingredients:
1 pound ground beef
1 tablespoon butter, melt
1 tablespoon taco seasoning
10 ounces canned diced tomatoes
4 ounces cream cheese
2 cups chicken broth
Salt and pepper to taste
2 tablespoons Cheddar cheese, shredded to garnish
Cilantro to garnish

Directions:
1. Place a skillet with butter and beef over medium heat. Cook until brown and transfer into the Crock Pot.
2. Add the rest of the ingredients except Cheddar and cilantro, and mix well.
3. Close the lid. Set the pot on Low and cook for 6 hours.
4. Ladle into soup bowls and serve garnished with Cheddar and cilantro.

Nutritional Information (Per Serving)
Calories: 396
Fat: 21.8g
Sat Fat: 11.7g
Carbohydrates: 7g
Fiber: 0.9g
Sugar: 3g
Protein: 40.5g

Bacon Soup

Servings: 6
Cooking Time: 6 hours
Ingredients:
2 tablespoons butter
4 medium jalapeño peppers, seeded and chopped
1 teaspoon dried thyme, crushed
½ teaspoon ground cumin
½ teaspoon ground coriander
3½ cups chicken broth
6 ounces cheddar cheese, shredded
Salt and pepper to taste
2 bacon slices, cooked and chopped

Directions:
1. In a soup pan, melt butter over medium heat. Add jalapeño peppers, and sauté for about 1–2 minutes. Transfer to the Crock Pot.
2. Add the herbs and chicken broth, and stir.
3. Close the lid. Set the pot on Low and cook for 6 hours.
4. Blend with an immersion blender until smooth.
5. Stir in cheddar cheese, heavy cream, salt, and pepper. Cover and cook on High for 20-30 minutes.
6. Serve hot with a topping of bacon.

Nutritional Information (Per Serving)
Calories: 210
Fat: 16.9g
Sat Fat: 9.5g
Carbohydrates: 1.9g
Fiber: 0.5g
Sugar: 0.9g
Protein: 12.5g

Chicken Noodle Soup

Servings: 6
Cooking Time: 6 hours
Ingredients:
3 tablespoons coconut oil
1½ cups celery, chopped
9 green onions, green parts only, chopped
1½ pounds chicken thighs, skinless, boneless
9 cups chicken stock
¾ teaspoon dried oregano
1 teaspoon dried basil
3 cups spiralized daikon noodles
Freshly ground pepper to taste

Directions:
1. Using a spiralizer, make noodles of the daikon. Use 3 cups of the daikon noodles.
2. Place a skillet with oil over medium heat. Add chicken and cook until brown on both sides. Transfer into the Crock Pot.
3. Add the rest of the ingredients except daikon noodles and stir.
4. Close the lid. Set the pot on Low and cook for 6 hours.
5. When done, remove the chicken with a slotted spoon and place it on your work area. When cool enough to handle, shred the chicken with a pair of forks and add it back into the pot. Stir and heat thoroughly.
6. Add noodles and stir.
7. Ladle into soup bowls and serve.

Nutritional Information (Per Serving)
Calories: 330
Fat: 24.7g
Sat Fat: 11.1g
Carbohydrates: 4.6g
Fiber: 1.6g
Sugar: 2.4g
Protein: 22.1g

Sodium: 1259mg

CHAPTER EIGHT

Snacks and Dessert

Mushroom Dip

Servings: 10
Cooking Time: 2–3 hours
Ingredients:
1 pound fresh mushrooms, finely chopped
1 small onion, finely diced
3 cloves garlic, minced
1 cup cream cheese, softened
½ cup sour cream
¼ cup mayonnaise
1 cup grated Parmesan cheese
½ teaspoon dried thyme
½ teaspoon dried rosemary
¼ teaspoon black pepper
½ teaspoon salt
2 tablespoons olive oil

Directions:
1. In a skillet, heat the olive oil over medium heat. Add the mushrooms, onions, and garlic. Sauté until the onions become translucent. Remove from heat and set aside.
2. Add the remaining ingredients into the Crock Pot and stir.
3. Add the sautéed mushroom mixture to the pot. Stir to combine.
4. Close the lid. Set the pot on Low and cook for 2–3 hours.
5. Serve warm with toasted bread or crackers.

Nutritional Information (Per Serving)
Calories: 216

Fat: 18.5g
Sat Fat: 7.7g
Carbohydrates: 5.3g
Fiber: 1.2g
Sugar: 2.1g
Protein: 7.4g
Sodium: 401mg

Artichoke and Spinach Dip

Servings: 20
Cooking Time: 4 hours
Ingredients:

1 package frozen spinach, thawed and with all the liquid squeezed out

1 can artichoke hearts, drained and chopped into quarters

½ cup sour cream

½ cup Alfredo sauce

Salt and pepper to taste

1 cup shredded Swiss cheese

Directions:

1. Mix all the ingredients in a Crock Pot.
2. Cook for 4 hours on High.
3. Serve with French bread cubes or cut vegetables.

Nutritional Information (Per Serving)
Calories: 59
Fat: 4.2g
Sat Fat: 2.2g
Carbohydrates: 3g
Fiber: 0.5g
Sugar: 0.2g
Protein: 2.6g
Sodium: 209mg

Buffalo Chicken Wings

Servings: 8
Cooking Time: 4–5 hours
Ingredients:
1½ pounds chicken wings
1 tablespoon butter, melted
⅓ cup Ranch dressing
12 ounces chicken wing sauce
1 teaspoon hot sauce or to taste

Directions:
1. Add butter, chicken wing sauce, and hot sauce into the Crock Pot and mix well.
2. Add chicken wings and stir until well-coated.
3. Close the lid. Set the pot on Low and cook for 4–5 hours or on High for 2–2½ hours.
4. Serve hot or warm with blue cheese dressing.

Nutritional Information (Per Serving)
Calories: 218
Fat: 15g
Sat Fat: 4.7g
Carbohydrates: 3.6g
Fiber: 0g
Sugar: 0.3g
Protein: 15.9g
Sodium: 1216mg

Buffalo Chicken Dip

Servings: 6
Cooking Time: 1½ hours
Ingredients:
4 ounces cream cheese, softened, cubed
1 cup mozzarella cheese, shredded
2 ounces blue cheese, crumbled
1½ cups deli rotisserie chicken, diced
½ cup sour cream
½ tablespoon Ranch seasoning
2 tablespoons jalapeños (optional), to top
2 green onions, thinly sliced + extra to garnish
½ cup hot sauce + extra to serve

Directions:
1. Spray the inside of the Crock Pot with cooking spray.
2. Add all the ingredients into the Crock Pot and mix well.
3. Close the lid. Set the pot on High and cook for 1½ hours.
4. Serve warm garnished with jalapeños, hot sauce, and green onions.
5. Serve with celery sticks or crackers.

Nutritional Information (Per Serving)
Calories: 232
Fat: 17.8g
Sat Fat: 9.9g
Carbohydrates: 3.5g
Fiber: 0.2g
Sugar: 0.8g
Protein: 15.4g
Sodium: 940mg

Lemon Garlic Chicken Kebabs

Servings: 4
Cooking Time: 3–4 hours
Ingredients:
¾ pound chicken thighs, skinless, boneless, cut into 2-inch pieces
1 tablespoon garlic, minced
½ teaspoon salt
3 tablespoons fresh lemon juice
½ teaspoon dried oregano
3 tablespoons olive oil
4 bamboo skewers

Directions:
1. Add all the cooking ingredients except chicken into a zip lock bag and shake well.
2. Add chicken and shake well. Let it marinate for 60–90 minutes.
3. Trim the bamboo skewers to fit into your Crock Pot. Thread the chicken onto the skewers.
4. Place in the Crock Pot. Cover and set the pot on High.
5. Cook for 3–4 hours. Check after 3 hours of cooking.

Nutritional Information (Per Serving)
Calories: 261
Fat: 22.6g
Sat Fat: 4.6g
Carbohydrates: 1.1g
Fiber: 0.2g
Sugar: 0.3g
Protein: 14.5g
Sodium: 458mg

Mushrooms in Wine Sauce

Servings: 10
Cooking Time: 8 hours
Ingredients:
2 cups chicken broth
½ cup red wine
½ teaspoon garlic powder
½ teaspoon Worcestershire sauce
2 pounds fresh mushrooms
2 tablespoons butter, melt

Directions:
1. Place the mushrooms in the bottom of the Crock Pot.
2. Pour in the liquids, Worcestershire sauce, and garlic powder. Stir to combine.
3. Add the butter.
4. Cook for 8 hours on Low.

Nutritional Information (Per Serving)
Calories: 58
Fat: 2.8g
Sat Fat: 1.5g
Carbohydrates: 3.7g
Fiber: 0.9g
Sugar: 1.9g
Protein: 3.9g
Sodium: 178mg

Apple Cake

Servings: 8
Cooking Time: 2½ hours
Ingredients:
2 cups white flour
½ cup brown sugar
2 teaspoons cinnamon
1 teaspoon baking soda
½ teaspoon baking powder
Dash of salt
Dash of cloves
1 cup applesauce
½ cup buttermilk
⅓ cup butter
2 tablespoons vanilla
1 large egg
2 cups chopped dried apple
2 cups whipped topping

Directions:
1. Coat a Crock Pot with a nonstick spray.
2. Line the bottom and sides with parchment paper, leaving a bit on top to lift out the cake.
3. Coat the parchment paper with the nonstick spray.
4. Stir together all the dry ingredients and spices in a bowl.
5. Melt the butter in a saucepan.
6. In another bowl, stir together the melted butter, applesauce, egg, buttermilk, and vanilla.
7. Add the applesauce mixture to the flour, and mix thoroughly for a smooth batter.
8. Stir in the dried apples.
9. Transfer the batter into the Crock Pot and level out the top.
10. Cook for 2½ hours on High.
11. Slice the cake, and serve warm with whipped topping.

Nutritional Information (Per Serving)

Calories: 323
Fat: 12.2g
Sat Fat: 7.3g
Carbohydrates: 47.6g
Fiber: 2.9g
Sugar: 20.2g
Protein: 5.3g
Sodium: 282mg

Pumpkin Custard

Servings: 6
Cooking Time: 3 hours
Ingredients:
15 ounces pumpkin puree
4 eggs, beaten
½ cup heavy cream
2 teaspoons pumpkin pie spice
2 teaspoons vanilla extract
4 tablespoons sugar
½ teaspoon salt
⅓ cup whipped cream

Directions:
1. Grease 6 ramekins.
2. In a large bowl, add all ingredients except whipped cream, and beat until smooth.
3. Divide mixture evenly in prepared ramekins. Cover them with foil.
4. Pour about 2 cups water into the Crock Pot. Place a rack in it. Place the ramekins on the rack.
5. Close the lid. Set the pot on High and cook for 3 hours, or until set.
6. Remove the ramekins from the pot, and place them on a wire rack to cool.
7. Serve warm or cold with a topping of whipped cream.

Nutritional Information (Per Serving)
Calories: 156
Fat: 9g
Sat Fat: 4.6g
Carbohydrates: 15g
Fiber: 2.1g
Sugar: 10.8g
Protein: 4.9g
Sodium: 245mg

Chocolate Pudding Cake

Servings: 8
Cooking Time: 2½ hours
Ingredients:
1 cup white flour
½ cup chocolate milk
⅓ cup sugar
2 tablespoons cocoa powder
1½ teaspoon baking powder
2 tablespoons olive oil
2 teaspoons vanilla
½ cup semisweet chocolate chips
½ cup chopped peanuts
¾ cup sugar
2 tablespoons unsweetened cocoa powder

Directions:
1. Coat the inside of the Crock Pot with a nonstick cooking spray.
2. In one bowl, mix the flour, sugar, and baking powder. Stir in the milk, olive oil, and vanilla.
3. Add the chocolate chips and peanuts. Stir very well to combine.
4. Pour the batter into the pot.
5. In the second bowl, mix the sugar and cocoa powder. Stir in 3 cups of boiling water. Pour the liquid on top of the batter.
6. Cook for 2½ hours on High.
7. Let cool.
8. Distribute the pudding cake into a bowl and serve with ice cream.

Nutritional Information (Per Serving)
Calories: 334
Fat: 13g
Sat Fat: 4.2g
Carbohydrates: 53.3g
Fiber: 2.9g

Sugar: 36.6g
Protein: 5g
Sodium: 12mg

Peach Cobbler

Servings: 8
Cooking Time: 3 hours
Ingredients:
4 cups peaches, peeled and sliced
¾ cup sugar
1 cup biscuit mix
1 cup milk

Directions:
1. Coat a Crock Pot with a nonstick cooking spray.
2. In a bowl, toss the peaches with ¼ cup of sugar.
3. Place the peaches in the pot.
4. In another bowl, stir together the biscuit mix, milk, and the remaining sugar.
5. Top the peaches with the mixture.
6. Cook for 3 hours on High.
7. Serve with whipped topping or ice cream.

Nutritional Information (Per Serving)
Calories: 176
Fat: 3g
Sat Fat: 1g
Carbohydrates: 36.3g
Fiber: 1.5g
Sugar: 28.8g
Protein: 2.8g
Sodium: 196mg

Coconut Rice Pudding

Servings: 8
Cooking Time: 6 hours
Ingredients:
1 cup Arborio rice, rinsed
1 can (13.5 oz) full-fat coconut milk
2 cups whole milk
½ cup granulated sugar
1 teaspoon vanilla extract
½ teaspoon ground cinnamon
¼ teaspoon salt
Fresh berries for serving

Directions:
1. Add all the ingredients except berries into the Crock Pot and stir.
2. Close the lid. Set the pot on Low and cook for 6 hours.
3. Top with fresh berries and serve warm or cold.

Nutritional Information (Per Serving)
Calories: 358
Fat: 17g
Sat Fat: 13.8g
Carbohydrates: 49g
Fiber: 1.2g
Sugar: 24g
Protein: 5g
Sodium: 150mg

Warm Fruit Compote

Servings: 10
Cooking Time: 6 hours
Ingredients:
2 apples, peeled and sliced
½ cup dried cranberries
1 cup raisins
1 cup dried apricots, cut in half
8 ounces canned pineapple, unsweetened
8 ounces canned peaches, unsweetened
1 cup freshly squeezed orange juice
1 cinnamon stick
1 cup slivered almonds

Directions:
1. Place the cinnamon stick on the bottom of your Crock Pot.
2. Add all the fruits and pour the orange juice over the top.
3. Cook on Low for 6 hours.
4. Serve with slivered almonds on top.

Nutritional Information (Per Serving)
Calories: 168
Fat: 5.1g
Sat Fat: 0.4g
Carbohydrates: 31.1g
Fiber: 4g
Sugar: 22.9g
Protein: 3.2g
Sodium: 4mg

Fruit and Honey

Servings: 10
Cooking Time: 4 hours
Ingredients:
4 ripe plums, cut into wedges with pits removed
3 pears, cut into wedges with core removed
3 apples, cored and cut into chunks
½ cup dried apricots, cut in half
¼ cup melted butter
¼ cup natural honey
8-ounce can of orange segments, no sugar added
8-ounce can of pineapple chunks, no sugar added
1 cup chopped walnuts

Directions:
1. Pour the pineapple and orange pieces, with their liquid, into the Crock Pot.
2. Add plums, pears, apples, and dried apricots.
3. Pour the melted butter over the fruit and give it a toss, then drizzle the honey.
4. Cook on Low for 4 hours or High for 2 hours.
5. Sprinkle with walnuts before serving.

Nutritional Information (Per Serving)
Calories: 248
Fat: 12.3g
Sat Fat: 3.3g
Carbohydrates: 35.2g
Fiber: 5g
Sugar: 27.2g
Protein: 3.9g
Sodium: 35mg

Conclusion

If you're looking for nutritious meals without spending hours in the kitchen, a Crock Pot is your ideal solution. I hope the recipes in this book make it easier to get that healthy food on the table! When in need, just use your Crock Pot.

Happy slow cooking!

Finally, I want to thank you for reading my book. If you enjoyed the book, please share your thoughts and post a review on the book retailer's website. It would be greatly appreciated!

Best wishes,
Lindsey Page

Check Out My Other Books

Air Fryer Cookbook for Beginners: 100 Simple and Delicious Recipes for Your Air Fryer

Instant Pot Cookbook for Beginners: 100 Easy, Fast and Healthy Recipes for Your Instant Pot

www.ingramcontent.com/pod-product-compliance
Lightning Source LLC
LaVergne TN
LVHW010300191224
799444LV00027BA/811